# Happy Working Relationships

## The small business guide to managing people and employment law

Simon Jones

Written by Simon Jones

Edited by Fiona Shaw

Design by Ken Ashcroft

Printed and bound by Lulu.com

ISBN: 978-0-9955594-2-4

Second edition published in April 2017

First published in January 2012

Wordscapes

The Mezzanine

Northern Lights Building,

Cains Brewery

5 Mann Street

Liverpool L8 5AF

www.wordscape.org.uk

www.ariadne-associates.co.uk

*For Trish and Anna*

*"For it is mutual trust, even more than mutual interest that holds human associations together...*

*Marriage is a scheme to accomplish exactly that same end."*

*H. L. Mencken (1880-1956)*

# Contents

# Contents

18. Happily ever after
Starting from scratch?

# Introduction to the second edition

Since the first edition of this book was published in 2012, there have been some significant changes in the employment environment, not all of it in employment law itself. But despite the changes, the overall objective of this book remains the same – to provide the owners and managers of small businesses and charities with an overview of their responsibilities towards their staff, and to kill some of the persistent myths and stories that surround employment law.

Probably the biggest change in the book has been the creation of a whole chapter on maternity and other family-related leave, following the introduction of Shared Parental Leave in 2015, but there have also been significant revisions to the chapter on TUPE as a result of the 2014 amendments to the regulations and recent case law. Other sections have been updated and clarified after changes in the law or feedback from readers.

Clearly, the UK's decision to leave the EU is likely to result in more significant changes in the coming years. But it's worth reiterating a point in the main text, that until 2019 the UK is a member of the EU and remains bound by its laws. And ironically, Brexit may lead to a more stable period of employment law in the next two to three years: in part because of the Government's stated commitment to retain existing rights; and in part because the Brexit process is likely to take up so much parliamentary time that changes in employment regulations are likely to be very low priority for politicians of all persuasions.

As always, the information in the book is for general guidance, and you should always seek advice from an HR or legal professional about your own specific situation. And, notwithstanding the point in the last paragraph, although the book is correct at the time of publication, you should always check that things have not changed if you're reading this book some time after the publication date.

Thanks are due again to Fiona Shaw and her team for applying their editing, design and technical skills to transform the manuscript into a book. And thanks are also due to all those who bought the first edition and made helpful comments and suggestions. Any errors that remain are of course my responsibility.

Simon Jones
February 2017

# PART 1

# The Dating Game

CHAPTER 1:

# The rules

All of us have, at some time or other, had a relationship with another person. It could be a husband or wife, a brother or sister, a parent, or just a close friendship. Making it work requires a bit of effort, and some give and take –from both sides. Compromises have to be made and everyone has to feel that they are gaining something from being in the relationship.

Most people agree that the two key components to a successful relationship are trust and communication. Without good communication, misunderstandings can arise, or we can fail to recognise that we want different things. When we can no longer trust our friend or lover, relationships start to break down and, in some cases, come to a complete end.

Once we get into the world of work however, many people seem to forget all this. Some bosses become unreasonable and dictatorial, acting in a way that they would never do with their friends or family. Some employees believe that they can demand certain 'rights' and behave in a negative or disruptive way. What both groups have forgotten is that employment is still a relationship between people, and the same basic principles apply to it as they do to friendships or marriage.

Business people often complain that employment law is biased in favour of employees, and their business would be much more successful if there weren't as many restrictions on what they can and can't do. Given this perception, it's interesting that most global surveys suggest that the UK is quite lightly regulated compared to most western economies.

But fundamentally, this view is missing the point. Time and again, studies show that the most successful and fast-growing companies are those that have happy, positive and motivated staff. They recognise that the law may set some ground rules, but that having a mutually beneficial relationship between the company and its employees is far more important.

When getting married, few couples spend time checking out the details of divorce or tax laws before making their decision. Similarly, while employment law is important – and much of this book will look at the way in which the law affects business – it should not be seen as the be-all and end-all.

Employment law in the UK is based on one very simple principle: that it is setting down the basic rules for a relationship between two people – the employer and the employee. Historically it's based on the principle that there's a master and a servant – the master being the employer, and the servant the employee. The assumption is that the master has more 'power' in the relationship, so the servant requires some legal protection. More importantly though, it's based on the premise that both sides have certain rights and certain responsibilities – this makes it different to other types of business law (like property and finance), which govern an agreement between organisations and 'things', like buildings, goods and equipment.

Of course, as with relationships in the rest of life, there can be different types of relationships with different workers in your business. And so there can be different sets of rules.

The most common group of people who work for you are your employees. These are people who work under a contract of employment. Employees have rights and duties to you – and you have rights and duties as well.

But not everyone who works for you is an employee. Some may be self-employed and provide you with a service – sometimes regularly but more often on an occasional basis. For example, a small company may retain a freelance bookkeeper to keep their accounts. Others may be 'casuals' – although they are paid through the payroll, they are only called in as and when needed – a relief receptionist in a hotel, for example. Even these people, who aren't your employees, will still have certain rights as 'workers', although they are far fewer than employees' rights.

It's important to remember this legal distinction between 'employees' and 'workers' – although throughout this book we'll concentrating on employees, it will be clear where certain things apply to all workers. Sometimes non-employed workers are referred to as 'freelance', 'consultants', 'self-employed' or 'contractors', and all of these terms are taken to mean the same thing throughout the book.

So, how do you know if someone is an employee or not? In 98% of cases it will be clear whether you have engaged someone under an employment contract or a different type of arrangement. If there's a dispute or disagreement then you should ask yourself the following six questions, as these are the tests that the law or taxman will apply:

- Firstly, who decides what the person will do and how and when they will do it? If you determine the conditions (e.g. they will work from your office, between 9am and 5pm) then they will almost certainly be classed as an employee; if on the other hand you simply give them a task (to complete your accounts for example) and they take the information and return with the task completed they are more likely to be viewed as self-employed. This is known as the 'control' test.

- Secondly, do you have an obligation to provide work and, if so, does the worker have to do it? If so, then the person is an employee – if not then they are self-employed. As an example, an employed accountant would be given jobs to do throughout the year and be expected to carry them out; you have no such obligation to give your self-employed accountant any work and he or she could refuse to do it if they wished. This is known in legal circles as the 'Mutuality of Obligation' test. There's one very important exception to the requirement on you to provide work, however, which is covered later in this chapter.

- Thirdly, how do you pay the individual? If you deduct tax and national insurance from any payments then the person is an employee, if, on the other hand, they issue an invoice and you pay it without any deductions they will be classed as a contractor or self-employed.

- Fourthly, how 'integrated' is the person into the organisation? If they are essential to the ongoing business then they are likely to be considered an employee; if, on the other hand, they can pick and choose who they work for and you could manage without them they are likely to be self-employed.

- Fifthly, who owns the equipment the individual uses? If you provide tools, a computer, office space etc then it is more likely they will be viewed as employed; if however the individual provides most, if not all, for themselves then they will be self-employed.

- Finally, what benefits do you provide the individual with? If you include them in medical insurance, pension scheme, or sick pay scheme then they're probably an employee. If it's up to the individual to organise these themselves, then in all probability they would be classed as self-employed. It's important to note that workers (whether employed or not) are entitled to paid holidays, so this aspect in itself wouldn't be a factor in deciding the outcome of this test. It also means that you may sometimes have a holiday liability to someone who is a contractor.

Normally, as a minimum there must be 'mutuality of obligation', and 'control' for a person to qualify as an employee. The more tests a worker passes, the more likely they are to be classed as an employee, although ultimately you need to look at the situation holistically. In other words, "if it looks like an employee and acts like an employee, it's an employee". It is technically possible – though unlikely – for the taxman to decide that someone is not an employee, and an employment tribunal to rule that they are (or vice-versa) but this is such a rare situation that we can safely disregard it for the purposes of this book.

The distinction between employee and worker has become much more important over the last few years. Some organisations have tried to class individuals or groups of staff as self-employed – for example couriers and other delivery staff. However, a series of recent cases has established that various such groups do have the rights of workers – most famously the ruling in the case of Uber taxi drivers.

For most businesses, the majority of people who work with your organisation are likely to be your employees and in this case you, as the employer, have certain duties towards them:

- You must pay the employee their salary/wages
- You must take reasonable steps to look after their safety
- You must pay costs and expenses incurred by the employee on behalf of your business

Employees also have certain responsibilities to their employer:

- The duty to obey reasonable and lawful instructions from the employer
- The duty to work to the best of their ability
- The duty to be 'loyal', i.e. not to compete with or damage your business

These basic responsibilities are seen as so fundamental that they do not need to be written into a contract – in legal jargon they're called 'implied terms'.

You may have noticed that there is no implied right on the employer to provide work for the employee to do. This might appear illogical – why would you employ someone if you have no work for them to do? It also appears to contradict the 'mutuality of obligation' test described above.

What it does mean in practice is that you can maintain a contract of employment during periods of a shortage of work (for example, if you needed to lay someone off temporarily) and also put individuals onto what is known as 'garden leave' (a term we'll cover in more depth later) if you want them away from your workplace but not working for a competitor. In the main, however, the assumption is that the reason for employing someone is that you have work of some description for them.

The cornerstone of the employment relationship is 'mutual trust and confidence' – that you, as the employer, believe that the individual will fulfil their responsibilities and that, equally importantly, they believe that you will fulfil yours. It's when this mutual trust and confidence starts to break down that problems begin to arise, as we'll see in later chapters.

This fundamental principle is the bedrock of UK law, but it isn't necessarily the same elsewhere in the world. This has two significant impacts on business – firstly, that if you're looking to set up subsidiaries or partnerships outside the UK you cannot assume that the legal framework is the same. More importantly however, European Union laws and policies have an effect on working relationships within the UK.

In some cases, the EU influence has been around for so long that it is an accepted part of the UK employment culture – for example in areas of discrimination/equal opportunities. In other areas, there is more of a drive towards 'collective' issues (between the employer and groups of employees), rather than the individual relationship which characterises the current UK model. Again, some of these are so entrenched in the UK, such as redundancy consultation, that they are seen as a normal part of the employment rules, while others, like works councils and working time regulations, are seen as somewhat alien to the way "things are done here". The final chapters of this book look at some of these collective issues and ways in which businesses can effectively manage them.

However, whatever your personal view of employment laws, it is a fact that all businesses must operate within the legal and regulatory framework laid down. Just as it is no defence when caught speeding to argue that you don't think that the speed limit should only be 30mph, it's no argument to say that you disagree with a particular piece of employment legislation, wherever it originates. As we'll see in future chapters, employment law doesn't have to be an unnecessary burden on your business and frequently can assist it. More importantly, it's only a small part of the overall employment relationship.

Obviously, at the time of writing, the UK is starting the process of leaving the EU. Two things are important here from an employment law perspective. Until the UK actually leaves, all EU derived laws and court judgments continue to apply. And secondly, the Government's proposed approach to leaving is to incorporate all EU derived law into UK law and then – over a period of time – review and amend it as necessary. This means in practice that UK employment law may not change radically during or immediately after the Brexit process. (Statements from government ministers and the recently published 'Brexit White Paper' have also suggested that changing employment regulation is a relatively low priority – although this of course could change with a new government or other significant political event).

As a final point, because employment is a relationship, issues are rarely, if ever, 'black and white'. Because of this, many business people find human resource issues frustrating, since there's frequently not a simple answer, and the actions you took on a previous occasion may not always be the appropriate response in the future. The derogatory description of people management as a 'soft skill' belies the fact that it can be the most challenging part of running an organisation – but equally good people management can enhance business performance and profitability far more than any other aspect.

CHAPTER 2:

# The thrill of the chase

Think about buying a car. A new one costs typically around £18,000-20,000, and, in deciding what to buy, most people would start by deciding what they need it for. Is it for long motorway journeys, commuting around a city, carrying lots of equipment, or transporting the family? Having made this choice, we might then identify a list of features that it needs to have – like two or four doors, luggage capacity, fuel economy – and some we'd like it to have, like a high-spec stereo or air conditioning.

Having done that, most of us would shop around, comparing different models and deals, and we might well get some technical assistance if we needed it – like a report from a qualified mechanic. Most people also would consider the 'hidden' costs, such as insurance, and tax. Once we had bought it, to get the best from it we would have it serviced regularly, sort out any minor repairs and only think about getting rid of it if it no longer fulfilled our needs or if the cost of repairing it outweighed the benefits. After all, a car is a major investment.

For most small businesses, the biggest single investment is in employing people. An employee paid £15,000 a year (that is, at the time of writing, only slightly more than minimum wage) is a major cost to most businesses, and by the time you've added in the time and cost of recruiting someone and the 'hidden' costs (National Insurance, additional advice on tax matters, additional equipment, desk space etc), to the salary costs, the total amount can be 30-35% higher than the basic salary. Yet how many people, in running a business, go through such a rigorous approach to recruitment they do to any other form of investment, or even buying a car?

A few years ago, there was a craze for 'speed dating' – spending two to three minutes meeting a potential partner before moving on to the next person and, in theory, deciding who they might want to date at the end of the evening from perhaps a dozen people they had chatted with. While it works for some, many found it a very dissatisfying way of trying to meet a future partner, because they did not get sufficient opportunity to get to know someone. Yet in the world of work, otherwise rational businesspeople will frequently claim that they can decide on a future employee on 'first impressions' or 'gut instinct'.

Getting the right people can take your business or organisation to the next level of success; employing the wrong people can destroy your business. So it's worth following some simple steps to minimise your chances of making the wrong decision.

Firstly, you need to be clear what job you want the person to do. While you may have an idea in your head, write down what tasks the person is expected to do (the job description) and the skills and attributes required (the person specification).

Secondly, you need to decide whether you actually need to employ someone to do the work, or would it be better to contract it out – rather than employ an IT Manager, you might want to contract with an IT support firm – or retain a freelancer (use a self-employed book-keeper rather than take one on as an employee)?

This decision might well depend on a number of factors – how much time do you need the person; how much the cost of employing someone is compared to the cost of outsourcing it; whether you need direct control over what the person does; and finally, how easy it is to find someone with the skills that you need (you will need to think where you can advertise the role to target people with the relevant skills).

Let's assume that you have decided that you need to employ someone, and have developed the job description and person specification. Before you go any further, if this is the first time you have recruited someone, then you need to take three important steps – if you already employ other staff, you will have done these already.

You must have Employers' Liability Insurance. This is a legal requirement – and has been for over 40 years – to cover you if a current or past employee suffers from an illness or injury as a result of working for you. This cover must be for at least £5 million and most insurers offer £10 million as standard. It is not the same as Public Liability Insurance (which is optional), which covers you against accidents suffered by customers, clients and other visitors to your premises.

Next, you need to set up a payroll system, so that you can make sure that the correct tax and National Insurance (and any other salary deductions) are paid by your employees. Most accountants offer this service (or can recommend a payroll provider) and their charges are usually well worth the time and hassle of trying to manage this by yourself. You can decide on the most convenient way to pay people, which will normally be by bank transfer. Note that employees do not have the right to be paid in cash, a belief that still persists, although it was abolished in 1986.

Finally, you need to sort out the practicalities of taking someone on – for example, do you have somewhere for them to sit? Do they need a computer or other additional equipment? Have you got male and female toilets? Is there a rest area where people can make a hot drink and take a break? Basic health, safety and welfare are not difficult for most businesses, and there is plenty of online help from bodies like the Health and Safety Executive (see the further information section at the end of the book) to assist you in planning common sense solutions.

You then need to decide the salary and any other benefits you might want to offer. If you've no idea what the 'going rate' is, then reviewing adverts for similar jobs should give you some guidance. It will also give you some help in selecting where to advertise. Including a salary 'range' in the advert will give you some scope to negotiate with the successful candidate when deciding to appoint.

Since 2012, it has been a requirement for all employers to enrol the vast majority of employees in a pension, to which both you and the employee must make a contribution, although as the introduction date has been phased some smaller employers do not have to comply until 2018. So you will need to ensure that you have a suitable pension scheme and that you factor in the costs of your contributions.

CHAPTER 3:

# Lonely hearts

Having done all this preparatory work, the next stage is to ask – where will I find this person? In most cases, you will need to advertise. Here again, you have a number of choices, the main ones are summarised below.

**Job Centres** will advertise your vacancy for free, but do have their disadvantages – it tends to be only the unemployed who use their services, so if the person you want is working they will not see your job. Also there is a risk that a number of the candidates you shortlist are only attending the interview in order to protect their benefit and aren't really interested in your job.

**Traditional print advertising** (newspapers or specialist magazines) is less common these days, but still a popular method. It can, however, be an expensive way of getting your vacancy known – you should add on around 10% of the salary as potential advertising costs, even in the local or regional press.

**Internet advertising** is increasingly used, and there are now plenty of reputable general sites as well as a number of specialist ones. As most people now have internet access, the argument that these sites limit your potential applicants has declined, and the costs are significantly less than printed sources. In fact advertising online, and circulating your advert to targeted groups (e.g. through social media such as Twitter or LinkedIn) can widen your audience significantly. For some sectors – mainly, but not exclusively in the technology area – the internet is now the primary means of recruitment.

Finally, you could use a **recruitment agency**. These have the advantage that they will take some of the administrative work away from you, and can usually get you candidates to interview faster. The disadvantages are that they can be extremely expensive (their fees can be 20% or more of salary) and they don't always provide a particularly good service. For some professions (e.g. accountancy) you'll almost certainly have to use an agency, as this has become the accepted norm for recruiting in those areas.

Some unscrupulous agencies will respond to your advert by sending you partial CVs from candidates registered with them. Watch out for this trick as you may end up paying twice – both the cost of the advert and an agency fee. (You can often avoid this by stating 'No Agencies' in the advert).

## Catching their eye...

The next step is a well worded and eye-catching advert. Remember, this is a relationship you're entering into, so you need to make your vacancy as attractive to potential candidates as possible. You are also marketing your organisation to the wider world, so it pays to look as professional as possible. At the same time don't oversell the role – if you are recruiting an administrator don't make it appear that it is the most challenging and dynamic role in business. Think about what is likely to attract people with the skills you need – is it the salary, the working environment, the exciting nature of your business, the opportunity for career enhancement etc? Be careful also not to use any words or phrases which could be seen as discriminatory (which we'll come to later in the chapter).

And don't forget some of the important basics, like where to send the application to, or who to call with any queries. Remember to put in a closing date that gives people enough chance to apply without delaying the process too much. Applications by email are the norm these days, but a significant minority of candidates still prefer to post their application so you need to allow for this.

If you have the time and resources, it's definitely worth acknowledging all applications. Again, this is giving all candidates a professional image of your organisation. A job applicant, whether suited for your job or not, is a potential customer, so maintaining a positive image is important. Automated email acknowledgements are easy to set up and can also state whether or not you are happy to give feedback at this stage, and when candidates can expect to hear the outcome of their application.

Once you've got applications in, you'll need to shortlist. This is where your job description and person specification play a vital role. Your decision whether to shortlist a candidate should be based solely on the criteria you have identified for the job. So, if you have decided that holding a particular qualification is essential or that the person must have worked in the same industry, then you can reject all those who don't meet these criteria. It's good practice to keep a record of how you arrived at a decision – firstly, because candidates are increasingly being advised to contact employers for feedback on why they haven't been successful, and secondly if your decision was challenged through the Employment Tribunal process (again, we'll look at that later in the chapter) you can demonstrate that the selection process was fair and objective.

CHAPTER 4:

# The first date

At the same time, you need to decide how you will select the successful person, since a written application or CV will only give you a brief overview of the candidates. Interviews are the most common way of doing this and, since establishing mutual trust and confidence with your employees is essential to a successful employment relationship, it's more than likely that you will want to sit down and talk with them. However, interviews on their own are notoriously poor at predicting how well or badly someone will perform in doing the job, so it's definitely worthwhile looking at other options which can assess candidates in addition to an interview.

Some of the most commonly used are:

- Aptitude tests (general questionnaires which provide information on numeracy or literacy)

- Skill tests (which are job specific) or practical exercises. For example, candidates for admin roles might be given an exercise to show their proficiency in Word or Excel.

- Personality questionnaires - which assess different personality types and allow you to consider this against the role you are recruiting for. Someone who appears to lack attention to detail might not appropriate for an auditor, for example. Done properly, these can be expensive so you will need to weigh up the benefits of using these against the cost; they would not be appropriate for every vacancy. Beware particularly 'free' personality questionnaires from the internet – they are about as useful as those magazine quizzes that tell you whether you are a chocoholic or not!

- Presentations - these may form part of the interview process or be a standalone exercise. Again be clear about why you are using them – is it to test knowledge of the subject or skills at standing in front of people and talking?

Given these add both cost and time to the recruitment process, you need to make a decision on which is the most appropriate for the skills and seniority of the job for which you are recruiting.

As mentioned above, interviews can be a very unreliable method of selection. The key to making them more reliable is to structure them. This means:

- Preparing the question areas in advance, using the job description, person specification and the candidate's application. This doesn't mean asking everyone the same questions!

- Ensuring that the question areas are relevant to both the job and the specific candidate

- Keeping accurate notes of the interview

- Think about what answers you expect – are there key issues that you would want candidates to cover?

Other points to note when interviewing include:

- Ensure that your receptionist or administrator has a list of candidates and times of interview – nothing looks worse to a candidate than turning up to find that no-one is apparently expecting them;

- Ensure that you have a small, relatively informal room for the interviews. Pay attention to the practicalities – for example watch out for things like the candidate – or yourself – being sat in direct sunlight and blinded!

- Never interview alone if you can avoid it – you won't be able to listen and observe effectively if you're trying to take notes, and, equally importantly, if there were a complaint/issue about the recruitment process then it would become 'one person's word against another';

- Avoid questions that are too personal or intrusive, or which don't appear to be relevant to the job;

- Unless specifically relevant to the job, do not ask questions about the person's health;

- Ask open questions ('how?' 'when?' 'why?' etc) – the candidate should do more of the talking than you. Make sure that you probe the key points of their CV; ask for examples to back up the points they are making;

- Use 'closed' questions (ones that can be answered 'yes' or 'no') only to end a question area and move on to another

- Avoid asking two questions in one;

- 'Actively' listen to the answers the candidate gives – use body language to acknowledge points they have made and to demonstrate you are taking an interest in their answer;
- Have details of the terms and conditions of the job, and the job description, available.

Remember that interviews are about gaining information about the candidate, and deciding whether you and the candidate will be able to work together (and remember, the candidate is also making the same decision about whether they want to work for you and your organisation). An interview is not an opportunity to score points, trip the candidate up with 'trick' questions or otherwise make them feel that it is an ordeal.

If you do it properly, good recruitment interviewing is an extremely tiring job – but should normally ensure that you make the right choice.

## Making a good impression

One of the issues that concerns many small employers is that of discrimination law – and it is often in recruitment that issues around equality and discrimination can occur. It hasn't been mentioned earlier because following a thorough and objective process like the one described should make sure that you don't fall foul of the law. But it's important that you understand the key legal 'dos and don'ts', as discrimination is one of the very few areas of employment law (health and safety being another) where you can be held personally responsible (and fined) – not just your company or organisation. Moreover, individuals don't need any 'qualifying service' (see later chapter) to make a claim, so someone who has never worked for you could potentially make a claim.

Equality and discrimination don't only affect recruitment – they can impact on a wide range of employment issues. So you may need to refer back to this section when looking at other areas of people management.

In summary, it is illegal to make your selection decision for one of the following reasons: a person's sex or gender, marital status, pregnancy, race, nationality, ethnic origin, age, disability, religion or belief, or sexual orientation. These are known in law as 'protected characteristics.' Some of this legislation has been around for years (sex and race since the mid 1970s) while some has been introduced in the early part of the 21st century. In 2010, the many bits of legislation were all combined into one single Act of Parliament, the Equality Act.

This may sound like an onerous and rather politically correct list of prohibitions. But, if you think about it from a business perspective, when designing your job description and person specification, did you include factors like 'must be female/unmarried/heterosexual' or 'must not be black/Jewish/over 50'? Thought not!

There are a number of ways that discrimination in employment can occur.

Direct discrimination is where you treat a person less favourably because they are a member of one of the above groups. So making a decision that you won't employ a woman between 20 and 40, on the grounds that she might get pregnant and want to take maternity leave, is direct discrimination on the grounds of both sex and age. Thankfully, most employers, whatever their personal views might be, understand that direct discrimination is illegal and it is less common.

Indirect discrimination is a more problematic area for employers. This is where an employer imposes a requirement or condition which, although it appears to treat everyone equally, affects one of the above groups disproportionately. An example would be a bus company who want to recruit drivers who live close to their depot, and therefore exclude applications from certain postcode areas which they consider too far away. If, however, these excluded areas were ones which had a higher proportion of applicants from a minority or different racial background, then the company might be indirectly discriminating on the grounds of race. They hadn't intended to discriminate, but the consequence of their decision is that someone from an ethnic minority has a reduced chance of getting a job.

Unlike direct discrimination, where there is no possible defence, it is sometimes the case that you can defend yourself by showing 'objective justification' for your decision, policy or selection criteria. However, it's often a difficult defence to argue, and it would be more sensible for most employers to ensure their recruitment processes are robust and non-discriminatory.

A third type of discrimination is victimisation. This is where an employer treats someone less favourably because they have raised an issue relating to discrimination, or have been involved in a case under relating to discrimination (e.g. as a witness). This type of discrimination is rare in a recruitment situation.

Some of the less common forms of discrimination are:

Associative Discrimination – if you discriminate against someone who is 'associated' with someone who has a protected characteristic. For example, if you refused to employ someone because they have caring responsibilities for a disabled person (even though the individual concerned wasn't disabled) they could make a claim for associative disability discrimination.

Perceptive Discrimination – this is discrimination against someone who you believe to have a protected characteristic but in fact they do not. The best example is in fact the case that established the principle, where a group of workers (including supervisors and managers) decided that one of their colleagues was gay (even though he was not) and bullied and harassed him as a result.

The potential for discrimination can occur throughout the recruitment process, for example:

- A poorly-worded advert, ranging from the obvious: 'cleaning lady' instead of 'cleaner', to the less apparent: 'requires five years' experience' or 'recent graduate' could potentially be age discriminatory, unless you can justify why these are essential to the job.

- Shortlisting: if you base your decision to shortlist on things like the person's name, age, sex etc. rather than the criteria you've laid down for the role, then the chances are you will be directly discriminating. There have been a number of studies in recent years, in both the UK and US – most recently in early 2017 – where individuals have sent in two applications, both meeting the criteria, under an 'English-sounding' name like John Smith and an 'Asian-sounding' name like Mohammed Khan. In many cases 'John' is invited to interview and 'Mohammed' isn't, which exposes employers to a claim for race or religious discrimination – one which the individual would almost certainly win, since – if the two candidates both clearly meet the criteria – the only reason for 'Mohammed' not getting an interview must be his race or religion. Many large employers now take off all personal details before applications are passed to managers for shortlisting and, although this isn't always a practical solution for most small organisations, it does highlight the importance of using your job description and person specification thoroughly when you are making decisions.

- At the interview: it's the case that many employers are now scared to ask almost any question in case it is 'discriminatory'. While there are several obvious things that should be avoided – like asking a female applicant if she is planning to have children – if you can justify why the question is relevant to the job and you ask it in a way that all candidates can answer, then you have a defence for asking it. For example, if your role involves evening or night work, it would be perfectly OK to ask all candidates 'you are aware that this job requires regular work in the evening. Do you envisage any problems with this?' However, if you only asked this question of a female candidate who you knew had children, it would be potentially discriminatory.

- Even so, there can be occasions when what may seem an innocuous question to you is perceived differently by the interviewee. Asking someone what football team they support may seem harmless and a way of breaking the ice, but to someone from Glasgow it would be seen as a coded way of asking them their religion (Celtic = Catholic, Rangers = Protestant), and might lead them to believe that you were trying to be discriminatory on religious grounds.

As with all legislation, there are a number of exceptions to the general rule, which, although uncommon, do allow discrimination in certain circumstances.

Discrimination on the grounds of a person's sex is permitted to allow special treatment for women in connection with pregnancy and childbirth. It is also permitted where there is a need for a person of a specific sex because the job involves personal or physical contact, or to preserve decency or privacy (This is called a Genuine Occupational Qualification).

Discrimination on the grounds of race is also permitted for genuine occupational qualifications, for example, what are described as reasons of authenticity – like Chinese waiters in a Chinese restaurant.

Religious Discrimination is permitted in very limited circumstances, again where there is a genuine occupational reason (for example, a Catholic school can insist that its religious teacher is a practising Catholic, but can't insist that its maths teacher is).

It's permissible to discriminate on age grounds if there is a separate legal prohibition based on age – for example, certain types of driving licence are only available to those over 21, so it wouldn't be against the law to refuse to employ an 18-year-old to drive an LGV. There are also other very limited grounds where you can also use age as a factor – but it's worth taking professional advice in such situations.

It's worth remembering that discrimination claims in recruitment are still comparatively rare – and that many that do occur are blown up out of all proportion in the press. It's important as an employer to be aware of your responsibilities, but not to the extent of letting it give you sleepless nights.

On the face of it, the recruitment process described in this chapter might appear time-consuming and difficult, but there's a clear business advantage to it:

- Even for a basic role paying around £15,000pa, assuming the successful candidate stays with you for three years, you're investing £60,000 of your organisation's money (once you add on the additional costs). That's probably the biggest investment decision many small businesses will make, so it's important to get it right.

- Creating a professional image of your organisation to candidates at all stages is an easy way to market your business. Candidates will get a better understanding of what it is you do, and, if treated in a professional manner, will have a positive view, even if they don't get the job. Every candidate may be a potential customer for your products or services.

- Following a thorough and objective process will enable you to defend any legal employment claim more easily.

Having gone through the dating process, you've now met the person you want to settle down with, and the next chapter deals with the process of getting engaged and married.

# PART 2

# Love and Marriage

CHAPTER 5:

# Popping the question

Many good Victorian melodramas featured men being sued for 'breach of promise' – where a woman took them to court for failing to marry them after a proposal. While that no longer exists in marriage, in an employment situation there's still the option for someone offered a job, which is then withdrawn, to take legal action.

So before you pop the question to the person you've chosen to recruit, take a deep breath and pause. There are a lot of small but important steps to be taken, all of which need to be done before the individual starts to work for you.

An employment contract can be formed verbally by you offering someone a job – say over the phone – and the individual saying 'yes'. If you then have second thoughts, or something comes to light, backing out of the agreement can be costly.

So, as the employer, how do you avoid this? There is a simple way, which is to make sure that any job offer you make is 'conditional' – in other words, that it's subject to the individual satisfying certain conditions. The most common of these is 'satisfactory references' – something that will be discussed later in the chapter. There are a number of others, some of which are essential and others which are optional.

## Setting the ground rules...

Firstly, you must make sure that the person you want to employ is eligible to work in the UK. You can do this at any stage in the recruitment process, but for reasons of administrative practicality the majority of smaller employers only carry out this check once they have made their final choice. Every potential new employee, regardless of their nationality or background, must be checked, not just those where you may have concerns about their eligibility.

While you are not expected to be an expert on forgery, you must check for obvious signs of a falsified document – for example different names, dates of birth, discrepancies between the individual and their photo. You must also keep a copy of the document you have checked on the employee's file. In an ironic twist, Baroness Scotland, the Attorney General who introduced the rules governing this area in the early 2000s, was fined £5,000 for employing a housekeeper who couldn't actually work here. Her error was not that she didn't ask for evidence, nor that she didn't spot that it was faked, but that she did not keep a copy for her records.

So, who is eligible to work in the UK? The simple answer is that currently anyone who is a citizen of the UK or any other member state of the European Economic Area (essentially this is the European Union plus a couple of other non-EU countries such as Norway), or Switzerland, is eligible to work here, and anyone who doesn't fall into that category isn't. However, it's slightly more complicated in that certain people from outside the EEA area are eligible for work permits.

For example, if there is a serious shortage of qualified people within the EEA area then it can be permissible to recruit from outside this area (nurses being a current example). The Work Permit rules change constantly and can be very time-consuming and onerous for small business, so it's important to check the current regulations and procedures – for example direct from the gov.uk website, or a specialist consultant - at the time if you are thinking of recruiting someone who is not from a European country.

Of course, this may change once the UK leaves the EU, and it will be important for small businesses to keep an eye on the news for up-to-date information. But to reiterate, until the UK actually leaves (which is anticipated to be in 2019), you are free to employ any EEA national without requiring an additional work permit.

The documents that any individual (including UK citizens) must provide are essentially a passport or national identity card, or something issued by the Home Office to confirm that they have permanent residency or the right to work in the UK. If they cannot produce any one of these, you can accept two documents including a UK-issued birth certificate and an official (Government-issued) document containing the person's National Insurance number. There are other documents you can accept, and again, if in doubt, seek advice.

If the person cannot give you the evidence that they are eligible to work in the UK, then you can't employ them. If you did, you are exposing both yourself and your business to large fines and possible criminal prosecution.

The most common check after this, but one which is in most cases entirely optional, is receiving references – usually from previous employers but occasionally (and particularly with younger workers who have little or no work experience) a 'character' reference from a schoolteacher or family friend. Again, the concept of references dates back to the Victorians where they were seen as an essential requirement to assess the reliability and honesty of potential servants.

These days however, references are often of little or no value, even though they're still widely used. The reasons for this are many and varied – in some cases it's because employers misused them by giving 'good' references for poor staff in order to ensure they left their own organisation; in others because individuals found evidence of factually inaccurate or misleading references being given and took legal action against their employer.

As a result, many employers will only give what are referred to as 'factual' references – simply confirming that the individual worked for them in a particular role between particular dates. Other than as a confirmation that the information in the person's application is correct, this doesn't in fact give you much to decide on the suitability of your new employee. And since there is no legal obligation (in most cases) on a previous employer to provide a reference, some will provide nothing at all.

In the past, some employers would try to get around this by seeking telephone references. However, the disadvantage for you as a new employer is that if you withdraw a job offer because of a poor verbally given reference, you run the risk that the employee may try to make a breach of contract claim as described at the start of the chapter.

More fundamentally however, you need to consider whether you will gain anything helpful from taking up references. It's unlikely that the person providing the reference will know anything about the way your organisation operates, its culture or standards, so they are unlikely to be able to comment in any meaningful way on how an individual will perform with it.

Unless your industry is one of the small minority where references are required (childcare etc.), you need to consider why you are taking up references – is it because it's the way that things have always been done, or because they will provide you with useful information about your potential new employee that you couldn't gain in any other way?

With the increasing use of social media, many employers will also search sites like Facebook or Twitter to see what potential employees are posting. Since many job seekers will also be checking your organisation on the internet, there is no reason in theory why you shouldn't do this. And indeed, sites like LinkedIn were set up to facilitate professional networking online.

But you need to be careful as to why you are doing this, and what information you are seeking. Does it really matter that someone posts a drunken picture of themselves on Facebook? If they have met your criteria for the role, of what relevance is the individual's personal life? That's not to say that there may be things that cause you to have reservations about someone, but simply that you need to clear as to your reasons. Again, rejecting someone for something they have said or done on a social media site might expose you to a discrimination claim, especially if you could not give a proper justification for your decision.

In the recent past, it was also common to undertake some form of medical check for potential employees. In the main, this was done by a questionnaire, with a referral to a doctor if anything untoward was admitted, although some employers required a full medical examination. Since the introduction of the Equality Act in 2010, it is now no longer permissible to make employment conditional on 'satisfactory' medical status, as the use of medical checks was seen as either directly or indirectly introducing the possibility of disability discrimination. The only exceptions to this are when a health issue is a legal requirement – e.g. to hold an LGV licence to drive a lorry requires a regular medical examination – or where the medical is to establish whether an individual can do an intrinsic part of the job. An example of this latter would be a warehouse worker whose job includes heavy lifting. Here you would be entitled to ask relevant questions about manual handling related issues, such as back problems, but no other medical questions.

The final common pre-employment check is a 'Disclosure and Barring Service' check – still known commonly by their previous name of Criminal Records Bureau (CRB) checks. These are most commonly used in the public or voluntary sector but in fact any employer can ask for a 'Basic DBS' check. This will give you details of any unspent convictions or state that the individual has no convictions. The cost is approximately £50, and you need to consider how relevant the information is to your decision, plus the time taken to receive it, before deciding whether or not to make it a requirement. Most small employers don't.

The more detailed DBS checks – known as 'standard' and 'enhanced' - are only available to organisations that require this level of information, in the main those who work with children or vulnerable adults.

Finally, are there any other conditions that you need to confirm before you employ someone – for example, if they claim to hold a particular professional or educational qualification, do you need to see proof of it?

The way to protect yourself – whether you make the offer over the phone, face to face or in writing, is to use the phrase 'subject to…'. So your phone conversation might go along the lines of:

'Hello, Ms X, I'm ringing about your interview for Office Manager last week. Subject to proof of your eligibility to work in the UK, and your NVQ in Office Administration, we'd like to offer you the job at a salary of £y…'

If you do make the offer verbally, follow it up in writing, confirming the details, as soon as possible.

All new employees are entitled to a written statement of their basic terms and conditions, which they must receive within eight weeks of commencing employment (although it's good practice to provide it to them on their first day). This is the document that is commonly referred to as the 'contract' although in fact an employment contract is made up of any documents that refer to terms and conditions, and may also include unwritten agreements or arrangements that have been established 'by custom and practice' – in other words, things that just happen continually which neither you or the employee challenges (as an example, if you allow employees to leave early every Friday, this can become a contractual condition even though nothing is ever written down).

The written statement must include the following pieces of information:

- your name and your employee's name
- the employee's job title or a brief job description
- the date when employment began (if someone has moved jobs within your organisation, you also need to state the date of 'Continuous employment' which is the original start date)
- pay rate and when the employee will be paid (e.g. weekly/monthly)
- hours of work
- holiday entitlement
- Where the employee will be working (if they are based in more than one place it should say this along with your employer's address). If the employee is required to work outside the UK for periods of more than one month then you must explicitly state this
- sick pay arrangements
- notice periods
- information about disciplinary and grievance procedures
- any collective agreements (see below) that affect employment terms or conditions
- pensions and pension schemes
- if the individual is not a permanent employee how long employment is expected to continue, or if a fixed term worker the date employment will end

A 'collective agreement' is an agreement on terms and conditions that is often negotiated or agreed across a whole company or even an industry. It is most commonly found these days in the public sector, but certain very large firms may also have them. Examples might be a nationally agreed pay structure, or a procedure for dealing with industrial disputes. Smaller organisations on the whole do not have collective agreements, although some (often in the voluntary sector) may adopt elements of such collective agreements – for example, many charities will base salaries on local government pay scales.

You can of course include other contractual conditions in the main statement – one of the most common being a 'probationary period' of three or six months. Probationary periods have no legal status and are purely a contractual condition – you do not gain any extra benefits and employees don't lose any legal rights they may have just because they are in a probationary period. It is purely setting down a point where you will make a decision about continued employment.

Other things you may want to include in the main statement are clauses about confidentiality, or restrictions on working for a competitor, for instance. These last are called 'restrictive covenants' and must be proportionate to protecting your organisation – you can't prevent someone from earning a living. If you do want to include them, it's worth taking advice to ensure they are worded correctly.

You may also have a staff handbook, which lays down company rules and procedures. This should not form part of the contract (and should state this explicitly) but will give the new employee information on things like what expenses can be claimed and how to claim them; what to do if they are called up for jury service; if and how they are allowed to work from home; general standards of behaviour.

The reason the handbook should be non-contractual is that it often contains rules that you may need to change at short notice. Contractual changes require a period of consultation and notice, which is nonsensical if you simply need to alter a rule about how employees book a train ticket for a business meeting.

Talk of 'rules' and 'procedures' suggests that you need to have employees working in a very regimented and inflexible way. This isn't the case. What you need to do is set down some 'ground rules' – which you can tailor to your organisation. Many companies operate with very few procedures and rely on the working relationship and good sense of their managers and staff.

## Planning the big day...

This leads on to the issue of organisational culture and induction. 'Culture' is often seen as some sort of mysterious management speak, but one of the most famous definitions is that given by American management guru Tom Peters as 'the way we do things round here'. So your organisation may operate a relaxed dress code or insist people wear formal business dress; people may socialise after work or hurry home and never see each other outside work; you may operate to very clear rules and procedures or allow individuals to make their own decisions. You may be very cost conscious company or heavily sales-driven. Even two organisations in the same sector can have radically different cultures.

In any small organisation, much of the culture is defined by you as the owner/ senior manager. So if you are personally keen on high standards of customer service, then this will impact on the organisational culture; if you work long hours, this will influence the way your staff operate and often lead to people doing the same.

With a new employee, it is important that you get them into the way your organisation works as quickly as possible. That way they will both become more effective in their specific job and build the working relationship with you. A good induction plan is therefore not a luxury but essential to creating this.

Induction is not simply spending a couple of hours getting your new employee's bank details so you can pay them, telling them where the fire exits are and giving them a quick tour of the workplace – important though those things are. A properly structured induction will cover things like:

- What are the key work priorities that the person needs to get involved in?
- What procedures/protocols do they need to know (e.g. cash handling, purchase orders, how to use the company's IT systems)?
- Which other people do they need to meet (key work colleagues/suppliers/ customers) and when?
- What knowledge of the organisation do they need?
- Are there any other areas where they will need training/briefing?

Within this process – which depending on the organisation and the type of job may take a few days, a few weeks or even two to three months – you need to build in time to review how the individual is settling in and whether there are specific points they need to improve or learn more about.

One very useful idea, if you can do it, is to assign your new employee a 'buddy' for the first few weeks, who will be available to them to answer questions. These include all the apparently insignificant issues that can actually matter a lot to someone new – like 'where's the best place to get a sandwich at lunchtime?', 'Do people make their own tea and coffee or do we make it for others on a rota?',

'Can you remind me who I ask about petty cash?' and 'I need to send these documents by courier – do I organise that myself or does someone do it for me?'

Starting your new employee is not just a whole load of paperwork. It's about the beginning of a new working relationship, with someone who you have just selected from a group of other candidates. While it is not exactly a 'honeymoon', it is the point at which you either start a serious long-term relationship, or – if handled badly – where one or other of you may think you have made a disastrous mistake!

CHAPTER 6:

# Making things work

Your new staff member is on board – you've completed all the legal formalities and now it's down to making the relationship work, keeping the individual motivated and getting good quality work from them. The thing is – how do you do it?

It probably comes as no surprise that there is no one way to achieve this. As has been made clear from the start of this book, everyone's different and can't be managed at the 'touch of a button'. Just as importantly, you, as a manager, will differ in the way you relate to people. So the first question you need to consider is – what sort of manager am I?

There are a considerable number of management theories around, and this is not a management textbook. However, it's useful to look at a couple of the simpler and most well-known theories as a way of identifying how you will manage and relate to your employees.

Do you think people inherently dislike work? And try to get away with the minimum possible? That the only way to get them to work effectively is to have strict rules and processes, and to motivate them with some form of cash incentive? If so, then you're a 'Theory X' manager.

Theory X managers tend to distrust employees and use threats and sanctions to get people to do their job. If something goes wrong, they are most likely to blame the person doing it rather than asking why it occurred.

On the other hand, if you take the view that people actually enjoy work and get a sense of satisfaction from it, and want to develop themselves to their maximum potential, then you are a 'Theory Y' manager.

Theory Y managers try to create working conditions where people can develop themselves. So they are more likely to support training and promotional opportunities and encourage open communication between managers and subordinates as a way of solving problems.

Of course, these X and Y types – which were developed by an American psychologist called McGregor in the 1960s – are opposite extremes. Most people are likely to fall in-between them. But it's worthwhile deciding which end you tend toward as a person, as this will inevitably impact on the way you deal with your team.

One of the dangers of this particular model is that the descriptions often make Theory X management appear 'bad' and Theory Y 'good'. As a result, many managers who tend towards Theory X often try to disguise it. Despite this, it is still possible to find many organisations operate on Theory X lines – modern day call centres being a good example.

If you want to make a working relationship effective, there's no point trying to be something you're not. So if you do tend towards Theory X, don't pretend to be a Theory Y manager – but recognise that it is a style that can create a negative reaction in some members of staff (just as Theory Y is not always effective in motivating some staff).

One other management theory – which combines elements of the McGregor model and attempts to make it work in most contexts – is that known as 'Situational Leadership', made most famous in the 'One Minute Manager' series of books.

Essentially, this model rejects the one-size-fits-all approach and takes the view that effective leaders will alter their style to suit the situation. So, a manager might on occasions take a very directive style, but on others encourage participation and delegation. It will depend on two things – the nature and urgency of the task, and more importantly the attitude, skills and motivation of the staff team.

The key to situational leadership is knowing which is the right approach to take in the particular circumstances. Part of that learning is understanding when your preferred or 'natural' style is not appropriate, and you have to behave in a way that goes contrary to this – for example a Theory Y manager won't necessarily be able to be as consultative and supportive as they would like to be when up against a tight deadline.

Knowing how you're likely to respond to situations is a very useful start to managing your working relationships effectively, but it's only half the story. Knowing what motivates your team members is also essential.

If you were to ask a selection of people what motivates people in work, the answer would normally be 'money' (and that answer wouldn't just come from people who are Theory X types). However, this isn't always the case.

Think about it. If you're doing a job you absolutely hate for £20,000 a year, and your boss increased your salary to £25,000, although you might feel pleased about the extra money, it doesn't alter the fact that your job is still tedious and unfulfilling.

Again, a little bit of management theory is helpful here.

One of the best-known theories is that developed by psychologist Abraham Maslow in the 1940s. His basic model is that people have a hierarchy of 'needs', which have to be satisfied, in order. So people work firstly to survive – to buy food, obtain housing – and then to create security for themselves – save for old age, or obtain job security.

Both of these needs can be met by money.

Once the individual has met these needs however, they then look for social belonging (the fact that they wish to be accepted by others in their group), self-respect and self-esteem, and finally to develop themselves to their maximum potential.

## The honeymoon period

While money can play a part in this, these 'higher needs' (as Maslow defined them) are primarily based on the individual's relationships and psychology.

Another psychologist, Herzberg, put forward a similar theory. His view was that the things that motivate people and the things that demotivate them were not necessarily the same. So, in other words, the absence of something that motivates you does not necessarily demotivate you. He called this the 'two factor theory'. The things that give people positive satisfaction in work he called (unsurprisingly) 'motivators' – for example recognition, personal development, or achievement.

The other aspects he referred to as 'hygiene factors' – they don't motivate people but need to be there to make sure the person is not dissatisfied or demotivated. These included things such as pay, working conditions, other benefits, and job security.

In short, hygiene factors are what make people come to work, but motivators are what generate good performance from them once in work.

You may agree or disagree with these theories. Indeed, many modern researchers have put forward other models that appear equally persuasive. But the important point is that to work effectively with others, you need to understand both how you are likely to react to a situation and how your team member is likely to react.

## Learning to live together

Let's take a practical example. One of the most common issues that employers have to deal with is where a member of staff is not doing their job 'properly'. There is often a tendency for managers – usually in frustration – to decide that the individual is 'not good enough', and look for ways to get them out of the organisation.

However, there are a lot of good business reasons why you should try to turn things around before taking this action – not least the time and costs of recruitment, which we outlined in Chapter 4.

As a manager, you have a responsibility to bring performance that is below standard to an individual's attention at the earliest opportunity. Not doing so lets the individual believe that what they're doing is acceptable – making it far more difficult to tackle issues later if performance continues to decline.

If a member of your team is not performing to the standard you expect, then assess the following before you speak to them:

a) Is it a task that the individual should be technically capable of?

b) Did you clearly communicate what needed to be done, and by when?

c) Is the person's behaviour/attitude the root of the problem?

d) Is there anything in work that could be demotivating the employee? (Like things we've identified, including low pay or poor working conditions – equally, it might be that they are bored or unchallenged by their job, or having problems with a colleague).

e) Are there any external factors you're aware of that are affecting performance? These could be personal or family issues, but could also be situations within the company that have an impact – for example pressure of work, or conflict with colleagues.

Arrange to speak to the individual on an informal, one-to-one basis. Outline your concerns, in a non-confrontational way, and aim to try and conclude the meeting with the following:

a) An acceptance there is a problem

b) An understanding of the reasons why the performance is below what is acceptable

c) Agreed actions that you are both going to take

d) A deadline, after which you will review progress (e.g. one month)

Follow this up with a letter, memo or email to the individual, summarising what you discussed and the agreed actions. It's also sensible practice to put a copy of this on their personal file.

It's often helpful to make sure any agreed targets follow the 'SMART' rule:

Strategic – they contribute to the organisation's objectives

Measurable – there is some objective way to assess whether the individual has hit the target

Achievable – the person should be capable of completing the target in the time allocated

Realistic – there are no other business reasons (e.g. other work targets) which will prevent the individual completing the task to time

Timescale – there is a sensible deadline by which the person should have achieved the task

If the individual's performance doesn't show any improvement – or even gets worse – before the agreed review, then you should bring forward the review meeting.

At the review meeting, you should go over what was agreed and how the individual has performed. Make sure that, if you committed to do something, that you have done it. If there has been no significant improvement, and there are no mitigating circumstances (perhaps a required training course wasn't available?) then you should consider whether to move matters into a formal procedure (which might be the disciplinary procedure, which you can see in the next chapter).

If you decide to go into a formal procedure, you must be clear whether the matter is:

Capability – the person cannot do the job, despite all the support you have given;

or

Conduct – the person can technically do the job, but is failing to perform to the required standard.

Give the individual notice of the meeting (normally at least 24 hours) and remind them that a work colleague or trade union representative may accompany them. At the meeting, ensure that they can give their point of view and consider this before making a decision.

In the absence of any mitigating reasons, your decision would normally be to issue a formal warning, which should be confirmed in writing. Any specific actions and deadlines should also be confirmed and the individual employee should be reminded of their right to appeal.

Once any appeal process is dealt with, you should continue to monitor performance and – where appropriate – provide support to the individual.

If there is still no improvement (or not enough improvement) then the procedure can progress, to final warning and possibly even dismissal (see Chapter 11 - On the Rocks).

Whatever the circumstances, avoid being confrontational or accusatory. For example, a general comment such as 'You have a bad attitude' will make the other person defensive and possibly unwilling to co-operate. You should support your points wherever possible with examples, such as 'I was unhappy with the tone you used when you spoke to that customer' or 'You seem to be making a lot of negative comments about the company'.

Although it's important to monitor the individual's performance, you should draw a line between this and being hypercritical. Don't pick up the person for every little mistake, but look for examples of the types of error/issue that you have previously highlighted. Unwarranted or excessive monitoring of performance can be considered as bullying.

Sometimes, however, you might encounter the reverse situation. Instead of performing below standard, the individual may be a very high performer. On the face of it, having a 'star' performer should be a significant benefit to your organisation – and in terms of your overall business performance it may well be. But high performers bring with them different managerial challenges, especially in a smaller organisation where you may find that you are spending large amounts of your time keeping them motivated.

With a high performer it's important to understand what motivates them, and for you as a manager to recognise when you have reached the point where they've outgrown your organisation and you can no longer provide them with job satisfaction.

Many high performers require a constant challenge – as they achieve tasks and targets easily they are always looking for the next one. If you can keep providing them with these targets, great, but there may come a point where you're unable to. For example, it's no good getting your star salesperson to sell products you are unable to provide. Without a challenge – however high – performers can become demotivated and disruptive to your organisation – and you then need to move into managing poor performance as described above.

Even with a goal to aim for, high performing staff can provide managerial issues for you. In some cases, they'll feel their performance allows them to bend or break organisational rules, or they may become intolerant of colleagues who don't meet their high standards. While you may want to give them some latitude, letting them get away with behaviour you wouldn't tolerate in others can send out a very negative message to your other staff.

If you can't achieve their aims, and there are no opportunities to promote or develop them further, then it's sensible to recognise that their needs will only be fulfilled in a different – probably larger – organisation. Doing this allows you to plan for their replacement and also lets them leave amicably at a time that suits you both.

The majority of your staff will, of course, be neither stars nor poor performers. This doesn't mean that you do not need to manage or motivate them. Regular performance review is an essential part of effective people management and you need to spend time to do this properly.

In many organisations this is formalised into the annual or twice yearly 'appraisal'. Appraisal systems frequently become discredited for a variety of reasons, including managers considering them a chore; forms that read like school reports; and staff who don't see any actions arising from them.

In some organisations – most notably in the charity/voluntary sector – the annual appraisal is replaced or supplemented by a monthly or six-weekly individual meeting between a manager and members of their team. These are often known by a rather old-fashioned term – 'supervision' – but are in fact a very useful performance management tool. As another example, staff who work in sales are also frequently reviewed either monthly or quarterly.

If you think about it practically, as a manager you're constantly talking to your team members. You will mentally be forming a view about their general level of competence, and whether there are any skills they need to develop. You will also be giving them jobs to do and measuring how effectively they do them.

Equally, your staff will be forming a view of what you are like as a boss, how reasonable you are in your demands and how willing to listen to their views you are.

All that a performance review system – whatever name you decide to give it – does is to create a formal record of these views and opinions. As such the precise way in which it's done doesn't really matter, it's the agreed actions and outcomes that are important. So when you meet with your team member, there are several things you need to do to make sure the meeting is effective.

The key – as with recruitment interviews – is preparation. Before the meeting, take some time to consider the following questions:

- How does the person work with other members of the team, or customers?
- Does the person produce work on time?
- What is the general standard of work?
- Are there any other issues either positive or negative that you feel should be discussed?

Now review training and development... Here you should consider not only 'training courses', but also other development opportunities like working in another area, or involvement as part of a project team. You also need to consider both what the person needs to perform their existing job better, and their future role within the organisation – are they a candidate for promotion, or a move to a different work area, for instance?

Think next about their objectives for the coming months. What do you want them to achieve in their job? Follow the SMART rules above when you are setting and agreeing priorities.

Encourage your team member to prepare for the meeting too. Ask them to think about the way they want their career to develop, what they think are the important issues for their job, what aspects they do well and what they do less well.

When you get to the meeting, remember the following:

- Hold it somewhere private and make sure that there will be no interruptions (like phones);
- Think about the points you want to get over and how you're going to say them;
- Ensure there are 'NO SURPRISES' – don't save up good or bad points for the meeting. If you're happy or unhappy with a person's performance – let them know at the time;
- Beware the 'halo' and 'horns' effect. Someone good will still have weak points, while someone who you're not happy with still has positive aspects to their performance. Praise and criticise where it's warranted;
- The meeting is not a negotiation; if you cannot agree differences then both points of view should be recorded;

- Don't make promises you can't keep (such as promising that someone can go on a training course);

- The meeting is a two-way process – listen to the individual's views and don't get defensive. They may have constructive criticism about the way you act as a manager.

Ultimately, the key to good management is no different to making any other relationship work. It's about good communication between you and your employees – together with the trust between both parties that is the cornerstone of the employment relationship.

CHAPTER 7:

# Family dynamics

One area where the marriage analogy breaks down is that, as an employer, you're often in a relationship with more than one person. As we saw in the previous chapter, getting good performance from an employee requires an understanding of what motivates them and setting clear targets. But in a work context, you not only need to manage individuals, you may also need to get them working together as a team.

Why some teams work and others don't is a perennial question, with some very practical implications. The first thing that's important is to have the right mix of skills. A successful cricket team, for example, won't comprise 11 great batsmen – it'll have a mixture of batsmen, a wicket keeper, fast bowlers and spin bowlers and the combination of these skills will vary depending on the opposition, type of pitch or weather conditions. In a work situation, this means doing a similar exercise to that which we looked at in recruitment – defining what particular skills you need before you decide who the team members should be. So, when putting together a work project team, you may decide you need someone with knowledge of sales, someone with financial expertise, a good presenter, and a technical expert.

This blend of the right skills is important – but it's only half the story. Bearing in mind that we have talked throughout this book about people relationships, it should come as no surprise that the other half of creating a successful team is to get the personality balance right. How many times have you heard phrases like 'there's a personality conflict between those two' or 'she knows her stuff but is difficult to work with'?

How you get this blend is one of the most difficult management tasks – after all, you can't usually make people change their personality (although you can often get them to moderate aspects of it). Getting people to work together is a key managerial skill and requires you to understand not only where people can complement each other but also where conflict can arise and how you can minimise this – it's seldom possible to avoid it all together.

Much academic research has been undertaken over the years to try and find the reason why some teams succeed and others fail. There are two specific areas that we will look at in this chapter – group development and the roles people play in teams.

One of the first things that you need to consider is that teams have a 'life-cycle' – they are created, undertake the task they were assigned to do and then, once completed, disband. The tasks of course may be recurring ones – for example the finance department will have regular tasks like preparing budgets, dealing with invoices, finalising the annual accounts and dealing with tax returns, but they will still require different people to be involved and a different set of skills.

During this life cycle, the individuals within teams go through various phases, which were famously categorised by American psychologist Bruce Tuckman as 'Forming – Storming – Norming – Performing'.

Forming is where the team comes together for the first time. Everybody is operating individually and getting to know their new colleagues, as well as starting to define the task. Even in long established teams, if a new member joins there is always an element of re-forming that goes on as the group find out about the new person, and vice versa.

Storming describes the stage where the team members compete to define how they will complete the task, who will lead and how they will work together. It's a stage in which conflict and argument are to be expected, but the key to managing this part is to ensure that debate stays constructive and focused on the task to be achieved. Some groups never get beyond this stage and as a result, don't achieve what is expected of them.

Norming is the key stage – the team members agree what is going to be done, who is going to do it and how and when things should be done. In other words, they have an agreed plan that they are all committed to.

The final stage is performing – getting the job done and resolving any issues that arise. The team know what they are doing and, just as importantly, there is a degree of trust between them that they can rely on each other to achieve.

A team can't jump straight to the performing stage – they need to go through the preceding stages first. Why some teams get stuck at the storming stage, or never quite reach the performing stage, is a subject that has also been researched extensively.

Probably the most well-known is the theory put forward by Meredith Belbin, a psychologist at Cambridge University, based on research he and colleagues undertook in the late 1970s and early 1980s. He was interested in why some teams work well, and others fail and in particular he was very keen to find out why 'clever' teams failed (like why the Kennedy administration's Bay of Pigs invasion of Cuba was such a disaster, when Kennedy had assembled the most brilliant military minds in the USA to plan it.)

What he discovered was that successful teams had a blend of 'team types' – and it was the combination of different types that was successful. Teams failed if they had too many of the same type, or were lacking a particular team type to give them balance. Each team type brought strengths to the team, but also had weaknesses, and it was balancing the weaknesses of one with the strengths of another that made things successful. Belbin was keen to stress that all roles are equally important – something that needs to be remembered since (as with Theory X and Theory Y), some of the descriptions can make some team types appear 'better' than others.

One other thing Belbin was very careful to note was that the fact that he originally identified eight team types does not mean that eight people is the optimal number for a team. As his results found, individuals have a 'preferred' role, but can also take up easily a second type and on occasions even a third. Also, depending on the nature of the task to be performed, teams can sometimes work even if they are missing one or more team types.

Belbin's original eight 'team types' are as follows:

**Implementer** – these are the organisers of a team who are generally very practical and hard working. However, they usually prefer tried and trusted methods and can be resistant to new ideas.

**Co-ordinator** – they ensure that the team members are kept on track and that all feel equally able to contribute. They can however lack creativity and the capacity to understand the nuances of an issue.

**Shaper** – highly driven and motivated, shapers are the people who constantly challenge and look for practical new ways of doing things. However, they can become so fixed on 'getting the job done' that they are intolerant of others feelings and opinions and be impatient if things are going too slowly for their liking.

**Plant** – creative, intellectual and unorthodox, plants are also impractical and pay scant attention to rules and procedures.

**Resource Investigator** – if you need to know who to contact or where to get something, resource investigators are key – they are serial networkers and communicators. However, once the initial interest in a project has waned they will be looking for the 'next thing' to stimulate them even if they are still needed on the original topic.

**Monitor-Evaluator** – they will focus on the facts and the results, and are vital if you need data and information to support the work of the team. Because they are so task centred however they can be seen as uninspiring and lacking the ability to motivate or enthuse others.

**Team Worker** – very good at promoting team spirit and listening to others, team workers can however be indecisive under pressure.

**Completer-Finisher** – perfectionists who will ensure no details are missed, completer finishers can sometimes worry about irrelevant details and be unwilling to let things go or delegate.

Although it's a sweeping generalisation, certain team types do often tend towards certain jobs or industries. For example, many entrepreneurs are shapers, a lot of advertising and marketing people are plants, many accountants are monitor-evaluators, staff in 'caring professions' like nursing are often team workers and completer-finishers can often be found in engineering or quality assurance.

You'll also see from these descriptions that there is plenty of scope for conflict – a shaper, for example, could easily become frustrated by an implementer, or a resource investigator by a completer-finisher. Equally, too many of a single type can also lead to problems – too many shapers will lead to disputes over the right way forward; too many team workers may lead to a group with good morale but that achieves very little. However, if someone can move into their secondary role then these potential conflicts can be more easily resolved.

For example, if the managing director of a business is a shaper, and they are leading a team where a more junior member of staff is also a shaper, it's likely that during the storming phase of the group that the junior team member will let the MD take the shaper role and they will then take up their second preference – which might be as, say, the monitor-evaluator. Occasionally, someone may take on aspects of two roles – someone who is an implementer may also take on elements of the resource investigator role. Sometimes a secondary preference might appear diametrically opposed to the first preference – for example a plant may take up the role of completer-finisher. People – as we've emphasised throughout the book – are different.

So, how do you find out what team roles people prefer to take? It's possible to work it out by observation and experience though this is a very long-winded and imprecise way of doing it. If you want to find out a 'Belbin' team role, the most straightforward method is to use the 'Self Perception Inventory', a short questionnaire that can be completed online at a relatively low cost. Details are contained in the further reading and useful websites list at the end of the book.

The Belbin model is only one of many (though probably the most well-known in the UK) and you can find out information on team styles through a variety of psychological profiling methods. However, as we discussed in recruitment, you need to exercise caution when using such tools. You don't need to be an expert on psychology to use them, but you should be aware that of what you are buying. Some are properly designed and reputable, others aren't – particularly if they are free or very cheap and you found them via a Google search. It's always worth reading around the subject, taking advice or making use of a consultant who specialises in this area before deciding which type to use.

CHAPTER 8:

# In sickness and in health

At some point, every organisation has to deal with individuals who are absent through sickness. The occasional absence, though it may cause your organisation some short-term issues, is usually manageable – but sickness can start to become a bigger problem when it becomes frequent, persistent or long-term. This chapter deals with various approaches to managing sickness and keeping it to a minimum.

If someone goes off sick, you need to know so that you can plan to keep your business or service operational. So it's perfectly fine to set down company rules that individuals must notify you by a certain time (e.g. their scheduled start time), and that they have to notify you at certain periods during their absence (e.g. daily). These rules can be whatever you require to keep things running.

When an employee goes off sick, it's more likely than not that they are entitled to some form of payment. The legal minimum is known as Statutory Sick Pay (SSP) and is payable to anyone who earns at least the level to be paying National Insurance. If someone earns less than this, they can usually claim some form of state benefit.

SSP is not paid for the first three days of absence (with one exception, detailed below) and is then paid at around £89 per week (this is the 2017 rate but, like all state-related benefits, this changes every April, so check for the current rate). Employees don't need to produce evidence of illness at all for the first three days (merely advise you that they are ill) – after four days they need to complete what is known as a self-certificate (which can be a form downloaded from the HMRC website or one devised by your own organisation), and only after seven days' absence do they need to produce a medical certificate issued by a doctor.

Provided that the employee complies with these basic rules, you must pay them SSP, even if they break one of your own internal rules (e.g. by not notifying you by a particular time). Your accountant or payroll provider should ensure that you pay SSP correctly – as it can become quite a complex calculation (for example, if one absence is within 56 days of the start of another, the rule about no payment for the first three days does not apply). SSP cannot normally be reclaimed and so is usually an expense to your organisation (again, your payroll provider should alert you to the very limited occasions you can claim some or all SSP back).

Many organisations offer more generous sick pay terms (some larger ones provide for six months' full pay and six months' half pay) but you're under no obligation to do this, and if you do decide to pay above the legal minimum, you should set these 'occupational sick pay' terms at something which is affordable for your business. It's also important to be aware that paying occupational sick pay does not mean that these are 'entitlements' for employees, but maximum figures – something which will be discussed in more detail later when we consider how to handle problem cases.

The main issue for many organisations however, is not the direct cost, but the indirect cost of absence. It can result in lost production, increased costs (through the need to cover work with overtime) and a reduction in service standards. Consequently, most want to keep absence to the lowest possible level.

The approach you take will vary depending on whether you are dealing with regular short-term absences (the odd day off) or a prolonged sickness absence.

Clearly, you can't stop people being ill. But what you can do is to keep absences to a minimum by careful management and by tackling, if you can, the underlying causes. To do this effectively requires a combination of Theory X and Theory Y approaches (see page 31).

Problems with frequent short–term absences, where people are off with relatively minor absences (colds, vomiting, infections) are usually the most disruptive to any organisation.

The most effective way to tackle such absences is to ensure that the individual is seen by their manager immediately on their return to work. This doesn't have to be done in an overly formal or assertive way – you should take the opportunity to enquire discreetly and sympathetically about their health, ensure they are fully recovered and make them aware of any operational issues that have occurred during their absence. By doing this, you not only make the employee feel valued but also make them aware their absence has had an impact on the business and their colleagues.

If short-term absences start to become repeated, then you need to decide when you need to act. This will vary from organisation to organisation – some have very strict and inflexible rules (for example three absences in a six-month period triggers a warning) while others operate more flexibly. Whichever approach you take, you need to be consistent – it is very difficult to take action against one employee if they can point to another who has a similar record without any apparent sanction.

You should also analyse the individual's sickness record – do all the absences occur on a particular day of the week? Or around certain times of year, like school holidays? Or are they related to key work deadlines?

At this point, it's worth sitting down with the employee and discussing their absence record. Sometimes being confronted with facts like 'You've been off four times in the last three months' or 'You seem to be off on a lot of Fridays' can make people realise that their absences are causing an issue for you.

Ask if they have any health, personal or family problems which are affecting their ability to attend work – sometimes sickness becomes a symptom for other issues and sometimes, rather than being an employee who is taking every opportunity to be off, you may have a very conscientious employee who is coming in at times when they are still not fully recovered.

The assumption should always be that the person who is off is genuinely ill. Never accuse anyone of faking illness unless you have firm evidence to support this – and if you do, matters need to be dealt with under your disciplinary process (see page 62), not as a sickness issue.

If a health or other problem comes to light, consider what you can do – if anything – to assist. In the case of a health problem, you may wish to get a report from their doctor giving you advice on the nature of their condition, its likely prognosis and prospects for recovery. You need the employee's consent to do this, and they have the right (in most cases) to see the report before it is sent to you if they wish. If the employee doesn't give consent, you are then entitled to make any decisions without getting medical advice. There is more information on this process later in the chapter.

One thing you need to be careful of is that if an employee has a known disability and has absences as a result of this, these should normally be discounted when considering their absence record. For example, an employee with chronic arthritis should usually have absences directly due to their condition ignored. This doesn't mean of course that an employee with a disability will inherently have more sickness absence (in fact some studies suggest the opposite). We'll look more at disability issues later in the chapter.

If there is no apparent underlying cause, state what improvement you expect from the staff member and the timescale in which you will review it. This would typically be three to six months although there might be circumstances where you wish to make it longer or shorter.

At the end of the review period, if there has been an improvement you can close matters – if not however you may need to take further action. Some organisations have a separate absence management procedure but it is perfectly acceptable in a small organisation to utilise your disciplinary process to issue warnings, on the grounds that the individual's attendance at work is unacceptable, which might ultimately lead to dismissal (see Chapter 13 for more details on how to fairly dismiss an employee). Again this is not to suggest that the individual is 'faking' illness, but is simply not at work often enough to do the job you are employing them for effectively.

While this process will help you deal with an individual, you should as an employer also look at patterns throughout your workforce as a whole, as sickness rates can be an indicator of poor morale, staff feeling under undue pressure or as a reaction to poor management. Issuing warnings may help to tackle the symptoms (the level of absence) but won't necessarily tackle the causes. We talked in the recruitment chapter about seeing your employees as a major investment, so if things start going wrong it is preferable – and significantly less expensive – to investigate the cause rather than ignore the problem until it grows to a point where it cannot be fixed.

If an employee goes off sick for a long period, you need a different approach. There's no legal definition of long-term absence, so you need to take a view on the point at which you need to act. Partly it may depend on the illness – if someone is off with a broken leg you can be pretty sure that their absence will end at some defined point with a full recovery, and so you may not need to take any action; if someone has pneumonia you can be less certain and you may need to be more vigorous in your approach. It's common in many smaller organisations to use four weeks' absence as the trigger for action, but it's up to you to decide.

One thing you shouldn't do is consider the individual's pay position. If you pay, say, 13 weeks' full pay during absence, you don't have to wait 13 weeks to decide to deal with the issue. The trigger is when the absence begins to create a problem for your business. Equally, someone may have run out of sick pay, but because of a known situation (e.g. the broken leg case referred to above) you don't need to respond to the situation.

Obviously, anyone who is absent through a long-term illness needs to be treated sympathetically, and you need to balance this against the effect the absence is having when deciding how to proceed. One thing you may want to ask yourself is how you would like to be treated by your boss if you were off with the same illness.

A third consideration is whether the absence is considered a disability – in which case you need to think about any additional steps to deal with disability discrimination. We will look at this later in the chapter.

If you do decide that your business is suffering as a result of an employee's absence then there are a number of steps to take.

Firstly, keep in touch with the individual – how often and how you do this will depend on both you and them. You don't want to create the impression that you don't care about their absence; equally you don't want to be seen to be pestering or harassing them.

If the person is well enough to receive a visit at home, go out to see them, in part to find out if there is anything you can do for them but also to obtain their consent for a report from their doctor (as above). This report is to determine whether the individual is likely to return to work, when this is likely to be and what actions you as an employer may need to take to assist with this. If the person does not wish to receive a home visit – it may be that they are still unwell, or that they prefer to keep work and home lives separate – then write to them along the same lines.

If the person gives consent to a doctor's report, write to the doctor, enclosing the individual's consent form. Bear in mind that a doctor may take three to four weeks or so to reply and will normally charge you a fee for providing the report. You will need to ask specific questions of the doctor, such as how long they expect the illness to last, if there are any steps you can take as an employer to assist etc. Vague enquiries tend to get vague (and consequently unhelpful) answers from medical professionals.

If the doctor says that there is no immediate or likely return to work, you must consult again with the sick person – looking at options such as other work, part-time work etc. If the reason for absence could be classed as a disability (see below), you must also consider whether you need to make reasonable adjustments to allow the person to remain in employment. In addition, you need to make the individual aware that dismissal is an option if they are unable to return to work and you should at this point set them a deadline by which you expect them to return.

On the other hand, if the person does not give consent to a doctor's report, consult with them again – stress that you would prefer to take action based on a doctor's report but will do so without if necessary. If they still decline to give consent, then you can make decisions – for example whether or not to dismiss – without medical evidence.

In considering whether the person's illness is a disability, you need in the vast majority of cases to consider how it is affecting the person in work. The legal definition of a disability is a physical or mental impairment that is long term (lasting more than 12 months) and has a substantial adverse impact on the person's ability to undertake normal daily activities. For the purposes of this chapter, it is worth noting that many progressive or recurring conditions are covered by the definition – for example, diabetes, multiple sclerosis, heart problems, arthritis etc. Cancer and HIV are also automatically covered even if at the early stages they do not necessarily have a substantial adverse impact on the individual. Disability is not restricted to those who have obvious physical issues (such as sight loss or being a wheelchair user).

Discrimination includes both the concepts of direct and indirect discrimination, which we looked at in the recruitment chapter, but there's an additional one of 'failure to make reasonable adjustments' in relation to disability. These 'reasonable adjustments' may include things like locating an employee on the ground floor if they have difficulty with stairs; providing special equipment, or changes to workload or duties. The key word is here is **'reasonable'** – a large organisation that owns its own premises is likely to have both the resources and ability to make a change that a small organisation, perhaps working in rented offices, cannot. Nevertheless, the important point is that you must consider what you can do in the circumstances and if you can do something to make an adjustment you must.

This doesn't, of course, mean that you are required to keep someone in employment just because they have a disability. However, a disability does require you take extra steps to keep that individual in employment wherever possible.

If, having been through the full process no other options are not possible, and the individual has still not returned to work by the deadline you have set, then you may dismiss with notice, following a hearing as outlined in the later chapters on ending the employment relationship.

One final issue that many employers have concerns about is 'stress', which in recent years has become the most common reason for absence from work. There are two extremes to this – one is that employers worry that if they are found to be the cause of stress, they may be sued by the individual; at the other end, some employers will take a very unsympathetic approach to an individual who is absent with stress, almost viewing it as not a real illness.

Everyone suffers from stress at one point or another during their life, whether caused by work or factors outside it (family problems, financial issues etc). Sometimes work can be the major reason, or it may be one of many contributing factors. Technically, stress itself isn't an illness, but it can lead to a variety of symptoms that prevent the individual from working. Some of these symptoms can be physically very debilitating.

One of the most effective ways of relieving stress is to remove the cause of the stress. If this is work, then identifying what the problem is and, if you can, removing it, is the best approach. However, if what the individual is complaining about is the normal level of pressure that goes with the job, then you may not be able to make any changes. If this is the case, as an employer you shouldn't be held liable if the employee is dismissed or has to leave the organisation for some other reason. But never ignore an employee who complains of stress – to do so will leave you potentially liable if they later made a claim against you.

Unfortunately, a small minority of individuals will use 'stress' as an excuse to avoid facing up to situations they find unpleasant. It's not unusual for an employee facing an allegation of gross misconduct, for example, to go off sick with 'stress'. As an employer, you're not (normally) a medical professional, so you have to accept what a doctor advises you. However, simply being off ill doesn't prevent you as an employer taking appropriate decision for your business, although it may delay things. Just because an employee is not well enough to attend work doesn't mean that they can't come in for a meeting (and on occasions you may want to meet away from the workplace to facilitate this.

The Health and Safety Executive (HSE) has produced a wealth of material on how to manage stress at work, and its website is a very useful resource if you think you have a particular problem. But the three key issues if you do have a problem with an individual employee are:

a) Never ignore symptoms, complaints or warning signs of stress – the causes won't always be work but if they are you should try to address them

b) Stress can be tackled as any other long-term absence; if it's becoming a problem to your organisation you must deal with it (which includes considering dismissal if other options are not possible or effective)

c) Don't allow your own view of what is or isn't stressful to colour your opinion of the individual – people are all different in the way they react to situations.

Over the last few years, the issue of mental health in the workplace has become much more prominent. Away from individual cases you need to look at what factors may be causing stress or other mental health problems for your workforce, and if you can seek to reduce or eliminate them.

CHAPTER 9:

# When the going gets tough

Work doesn't exist in a bubble, separate from other aspects of life. Even though people tend to spend more of their waking hours at work than on any other single activity, they still have lives and families away from work (as you as a business manager do too) and will attach varying degrees of importance to them.

Sometimes, life outside of work will intrude on your organisation. This chapter looks both at employees' legal rights in these situations, and at ways in which you can manage your organisation to minimise any negative impacts.

## Holidays

Probably the biggest issue is when employees need time off during their normal working hours. Here, there are a variety of legal entitlements, many of which depend on the particular circumstances.

The first of these, which everyone is entitled to, and one which is so commonplace that you probably don't even think about it, is the right to take holidays on full pay. What may surprise you is that this did not become a legal right until 1998, when the UK adopted the EU Working Time Directive (of which more later).

Employees are entitled to a minimum of 5.6 weeks holiday in a year – that's 28 days for an employee who works five days per week. This includes bank holidays – of which there are normally eight in the UK. (In recent years there have been additional one-off holidays, for example the Queen's Diamond Jubilee in 2012). So if your business closes on bank holidays, an employee is entitled to a minimum of 20 days' paid holiday. If your organisation works normally on a bank holiday (in a retail business, for example), then staff are entitled to take 28 days.

Part-timers accrue pro-rata holidays – so someone who works three days per week is entitled to 5.6 of their 'weeks' – 17 days including bank holidays.

People accrue holidays during the course of the year, even if they are off sick or on some form of extended leave (maternity leave, for example). And they cannot opt to take payment in lieu or defer holidays into a future year.

Note that if you offer holidays which are better than the statutory minimum (which a lot of organisations do), you can agree to pay off or defer holidays. What you cannot do is stop people taking their statutory entitlement.

You may remember that in the first chapter we distinguished between 'employees' and 'workers'. Holiday – and every other aspect covered by the Working Time Regulations – is one of those areas that apply to both categories. So, if you engage a freelance individual for three months' full time work, they are entitled to take 1.4 weeks (seven days) paid holiday during that period. It's not uncommon in such situations to make a condition that holidays are taken at the end of the piece of work, although this may depend on how long the contract is.

As noted above, the right is to holidays on full normal pay. Recent cases have made it clear that 'full normal pay' includes things like regular overtime (even if overtime is 'voluntary') and commission/bonus. The principle is that individuals should not be penalised by taking home less money when on holiday than they would do when in work.

## Other entitlements to time off

Employees have various other rights to take time off work, though these are all unpaid, and they are all situations which occur infrequently in small organisations. Nevertheless you should be aware of them in case you receive a request.

The first – and probably the most common – is what is sometimes referred to as 'emergency time off to care for a dependent'. This is where an employee has an unforeseen problem with a child, elderly relative or someone else who is dependent on him or her. In this situation the employee must notify you as soon as possible and how long they expect to be off – although the right to time off is only for what is 'reasonable' in the circumstances. The purpose of the leave is to allow the employee to make alternative arrangements, not to take time off for care, and the guidance notes issued at the same time as the regulations that cover this suggest it would be a very unusual if this was more than one to two days.

So, a school closure due to bad weather, or an elderly parent being suddenly admitted to hospital would be the sort of situation that qualified – a school closure due to a teacher's strike where the date was known some time in advance, or a planned admission to a hospital wouldn't qualify for this emergency time off.

The second is time off for public duties. This is where an employee is a JP; a councillor; a school governor; a member of a statutory authority (e.g. a health authority) or tribunal (e.g. a lay member of an employment tribunal) and various other specified public bodies. Here, you must give people reasonable time off –

although what is reasonable will depend on the size of your business and the effect the employee's absence will have on it. So, while you couldn't refuse someone who simply requested a day off to sit as a magistrate, you could refuse them time off if it was the fourth or fifth time that month and they had also requested time off for some other public duty.

It's worth reiterating that such individuals are a comparative rarity and that you can agree with them in advance how much time off you are prepared to allow – one small business that employed a local councillor agreed with him at the start of his employment to allow 1.5 unpaid days per month for him to attend council meetings and if he wanted any extra time he had to book holidays (which could be refused) in accordance with the company's normal rules.

A third area is jury service. If an employee is summoned for jury service you must allow them the time off, although if the absence would cause you particular business problems you can request a postponement – it's up to the courts whether or not this is granted. Some employers do agree to pay if an individual is called up for jury service (since the allowance paid to jurors is very small) but you are under no obligation to.

Fourthly, there are certain situations where the government may call up reserve troops – this has happened in the recent past with both the Afghanistan and Iraq conflicts. In such a situation you must allow them time off. This only applies where there is a call-up – there is no such right to time off for things like annual Reserve Forces training camps etc.

In all of these situations, in addition to the right to time off, the employee has the right to return to work and not to suffer any detriment in work (for example, not being offered overtime that other staff are offered, or being passed over for promotion) because of their time off. Needless to say you can't dismiss someone for exercising their legal rights – this is classed as an automatically unfair dismissal (see Chapter Four).

In practice, almost all of these situations are better managed by coming to some sort of agreement, which suits both the individual and your organisation, in advance – so, if you have an employee with some sort of outside interest who needs time off, talk to them about it and come to some arrangement with them.

One area you may have noticed by its absence is compassionate or bereavement leave. There is no statutory right to such time off, but it would be an unusual and somewhat unfeeling employer who didn't grant an employee some time off in the event of the death or serious illness of a partner or immediate relative.

## Flexible working

Every employee has the right to request a change to their previously agreed or contractual working arrangements. The important thing here is that the right is 'to request' – so you can refuse a request, provided you have a valid business reason for doing so. Although every eligible employee can request this, in practice the majority of requests come from women returning from maternity leave.

To make a request, the employee must have 26 weeks' or more service and must not have made a previous request within the last 12 months.

You can legitimately refuse a request if it would add to your business costs, provide a worse service to customers, affect quality or productivity, or if you cannot reorganise workloads or recruit additional staff, or if there is not enough work at the time the individual wishes to work. In other words, the same reasons why you wouldn't make any other change to your business.

The individual can appeal against a decision to reject a request, and this should be dealt with in a similar way to a grievance appeal (which we'll cover in the next section).

While in some businesses the knee-jerk reaction is to look for ways to say 'no', you should ask yourself why the employee is making the request and what effect it will have on their motivation if you do reject it. It is better to think about whether you can accommodate a request in some way – and remember that a sensible discussion might lead to a compromise solution that works for you and the employee.

## Working time

The Working Time Regulations are another area which impact on the people who work for you. As we have already seen, they apply to not just to employees but to all  those classed as 'workers', and they govern minimum holiday entitlements.

The most well-known of the regulations is that known as the 48-hour rule, which many people incorrectly think means that a worker cannot work more than 48 hours per week. In fact, the rule is that an individual cannot work on average more than 48 hours per week, calculated over a 17-week period. So the person could work more than 48 hours in any one week if they didn't exceed that figure on average.

Adult workers (those over 18) can also opt out of this particular rule – though they cannot be forced to do so (or suffer any detriment if they don't). They can't however opt out of any of the other working time rules.

Adult workers are also entitled to a 20-minute break if their working day is more than six hours – which must be away from the work area if they wish; to a minimum of 11 hours rest in each 24 hour period; and at least 24 hours off in every seven days (although this last can be aggregated over 14 days, so that they could work for 12 days then have two days off).

Adult workers who work at night – which is defined as working at least three hours of their shift between midnight and 5am - are also entitled to a health assessment before they start such a work pattern and at regular intervals thereafter, and if the work is particular hazardous or causes physical or mental strain they have a right not to work more than eight hours in every 24.

Young workers – those over school leaving age but under 18 – are restricted to a maximum eight-hour day and 40 hour week (which unlike adults is not 'averaged'). They are also given enhanced rest periods and breaks, and usually are not allowed to undertake night work.

There are a number of groups of workers who are exempt from the Working Time Regulations. Unless you work in a specific industry that is excluded (like road transport – where there are separate rules on how long someone can drive for, for example), the most common one is where an individual has control over their own working time – for example, a director or senior manager.

One question that is often asked is why there are such restrictions on working time? The answer simply is safety – tired workers are statistically more likely to have accidents. But there are also some other business reasons why you wouldn't want to have individuals working excessive hours – including the fact that tired workers are unlikely to be as productive or produce work to a consistent quality. The regulations don't prevent you from dealing with a short-term spike in demand or some other business issue – but they do protect workers from endangering themselves and others through constant overwork.

## And finally

On the face of it, all these regulations seem to fit exactly the sort of 'red-tape' that many small organisations complain about. And if you take a very legalistic approach to managing them they can become quite onerous.

In the real world however, most small organisations are unlikely to have to deal with most on a regular basis – if at all – and, in any event, the majority of situations can be resolved by a bit of 'give and take' by the employer and employee. They are just a part of the framework that governs the employee relationship. Only if one or other party digs their heels in are disputes about legal rights, and complaints or grievances, likely to ensue.

CHAPTER 10:

# The patter of tiny feet

Going back to our analogy of employment as a marriage, in many cases – after a period of marriage – along come babies. So, this chapter looks at employees' rights during pregnancy and after childbirth.

For many small businesses and organisations, the words 'maternity leave' cause worry and concern. The prospect of losing a key employee for up to a year is understandably problematic, but, as I hope to show, proper planning and good communication can - as with many people related issues – minimise the potential disruption. It's also worth remembering that virtually all the parental rights outlined in this chapter only apply to employees, not workers or other freelance staff.

While, in the main, time off for parental reasons is still predominantly taken by the mother, you need to be aware that parental leave and pay can be shared between the mother and father. So it's entirely possible that you may get a request for time off from a variety of sources. And as a final caveat before we get into the details, although I have and will continue to refer to the 'father' in this chapter, it's important to understand that 'father' in this context means an individual who is not the mother, who has responsibility for the child – they do not have to be the biological father. However, parental leave can only be shared between the mother and one other person – and that other person cannot be a blood relative (grandparent etc).

The first thing to be aware of is that all pregnant women are entitled to up to one year's maternity leave. This is irrespective of how long they have worked for you – they could be pregnant on the day they start work.

A pregnant employee need not officially notify you that she is pregnant until 15 weeks before the baby is due to qualify for maternity leave. However, she does have the right to paid time off for ante-natal appointments (where you can ask for evidence, such as an appointment card) and as an employer, you have a health and safety responsibility towards a pregnant employee. You may need to carry out a further risk assessment which identifies any hazards that might affect her or her baby, so it's more than likely that you'll be aware well before this date. (Of course, many employees will tell you long before as well).

This magic date of '15 weeks before' is because this is the earliest date that a doctor or midwife will issue a maternity certificate stating the expected date of birth. As an employer, you are entitled to a copy of the maternity certificate as your evidence for granting maternity leave. The date of issuing the certificate is also the earliest date that a woman can give notice to begin her maternity leave – though in practice, many women work far closer to the date of birth. What she must do however is give you the date she intends to start maternity leave at the 15 weeks before date, and must give 28 days' notice if she wishes to change it. This is to allow you to plan for any maternity cover you require – which might be a temporary employee, reallocating roles or giving an existing member of staff a temporary promotion.

If she gives birth prematurely before officially beginning maternity leave, or if she is signed off sick for a pregnancy-related reason four weeks or less before the expected date of birth, then maternity leave begins automatically at that point.

An employee on maternity leave does not have to take her full 52-week entitlement, but if she wishes to come back before this she must give you eight weeks' notice. This is to allow you to give any temporary replacement proper notice. She cannot, however, return for at least two weeks after the baby is born (four weeks if she works in a factory environment) – this is known as compulsory maternity leave.

An employee is not necessarily paid during maternity leave - and if she is you can claim back some or all of the cost. If an employee has worked for you for more than 26 weeks at the magic '15 weeks before' date, (i.e. more than 41 weeks in total) and earns enough to pay National Insurance, then she will be due Statutory Maternity Pay (SMP). This is 90% of her full normal pay for the first six weeks, followed by a fixed amount for up to the next 39 weeks. From April 2017, this amount is £140.98 per week (unless 90% of full normal pay is less than this, in which case she continues to be paid this rate). As always with statutory benefits, they are reviewed every year, so check the current rates.

As an employer, you can claim back 92% of the cost of Statutory Maternity Pay (and any of the other statutory parental payments we will look at in this chapter). If you are a very small employer, this increases to 103% to reflect the additional administration costs. Your accountant or payroll provider will advise on how to do this.

Just like sick pay, you can, of course, pay more than this statutory rate. If you choose to do so, you cannot claim back the extra, just the SMP amounts.

If a pregnant employee isn't eligible for Statutory Maternity Pay, either because she hasn't worked for you for long enough, or doesn't earn enough, she claims maternity allowance as a state benefit via the Job Centre.

Although an employee on maternity leave may not receive her full pay, all her other contractual benefits (like a company car, health insurance) remain in force while she's on maternity leave. An employee on maternity leave will also still accrue holidays, but she isn't allowed to take them while absent on maternity leave. For this reason, many employers encourage pregnant staff to 'use up' their holiday entitlement prior to going on maternity leave (and many employees are also happy to do this, so that their maternity leave period begins as late as possible). It's a matter of agreement between you and the individual employee.

You can ask a woman on maternity leave to attend work for a maximum of ten days (which could be single days or two full weeks) – these are known as 'keeping in touch' (or KIT) days and can be used for things like conferences or training, for instance. You don't have to offer them – and equally the employee is under no obligation to attend if asked. If someone does attend a keeping in touch day, they receive their normal pay for that day.

Women on maternity leave have the right to return to work to the same job, on the same terms and conditions and with their continuous service retained. If, for any reason, you cannot offer the same job back you must offer something of similar status and on similar terms and conditions.

If you are in a redundancy situation (see Chapter 14), which affects the role of the woman on maternity leave, then you need to ensure that proper consultation takes place with her – even if she's not in work. However, a woman on maternity leave has particular protection in a redundancy situation; if she is suitable and competent for her existing role then she must be given it – even if you have employees who you are think are better than the job. This is one of the very few areas where the law not only permits but actually requires positive discrimination.

Maternity leave rules and entitlements have been around since the 1970s, and although they have been modified and adapted since then, there's no reason why employers shouldn't be aware of their responsibilities in this area. While the disruption to a business, particularly a small one, should not be discounted, the regulations do build in periods of notice, and this, together with proper communication with an employee and some planning, can help to reduce this disruption.

Where the rules have changed in recent years, most recently in 2015, they have served to give increased rights to fathers in such a situation. For example, fathers have the right to time-off to accompany a partner to up to two ante-natal appointments, although in their case, it's unpaid. And fathers have the right to take up to two weeks' paternity leave, around the time of the child's birth, provided they have worked for you for at least 26 weeks, 15 weeks before the baby is due. Such leave is paid at the Statutory Paternity Pay rate (which is the same as the lower SMP rate - £140.98 in April 2017) if the father meets the minimum level of pay.

One of the biggest changes in recent years is the introduction of Shared Parental Leave. At its simplest, it is what it says – both parents can share the mother's maternity leave entitlements.

Where it can get confusing is that the mother and the father may not both work for you. And it's probably easier to understand if we consider them each separately.

If you employ the mother, then things operate at the start in exactly the same way as maternity leave – she must give you notice in the same way and must remain off for at least the first two weeks after the baby is born (four in a factory).

She must give you eight weeks' written notice of ending her maternity leave (again, no different to any other early return from maternity leave) and that she intends to take shared parental leave. To remain eligible, she must also continue to be employed by you throughout the shared parental leave period.

She can then return to work and take further periods of Shared Parental Leave - for example returning to work for a month, then taking a month off; returning to work for a further month, then taking a month off. She can do this up to three times and must give you eight weeks' notice in writing of intending to do this. The notice is to give you time to plan your workload.

To avoid the need to constantly give notice, you can agree a pattern with the mother about how she is going to take her shared parental leave. If you do, she can still vary this by giving eight weeks' notice.

If, on the other hand, you employ the father, to qualify he must have been in work for 26 weeks out of the 66 weeks before the baby is born and to have earned at least £390 during this period.

The father must give you eight weeks' notice of taking shared parental leave, and confirm their proposed start and end dates. He should also produce a declaration from the mother confirming the date she intends to return to work and that he has responsibility for the child. As the father's employer, you can request evidence from the mother's employer to confirm that she has returned to work and what maternity payments she has received.

The father takes shared parental leave in much the same way as the mother – either by advising you of three separate occasions of wishing to take parental leave, or a continuous block, or an agreed pattern. It is possible for both the mother and father to be off at the same time, and this would use up the 52 weeks faster.

You can use 'keeping in touch' days with both parents – up to 20 days per parent, in addition to the ten that can be used with a woman on maternity leave. Confusingly, these are sometimes referred to as Shared Parental Leave In Touch, or SPLIT, days.

Very similar rules apply when someone is adopting a child – the mother and father are both entitled to a period of time off which may be paid (at similar rates).

In addition to maternity, paternity and shared parental leave, parents who have worked for you for at least a year are entitled to take up to 13 weeks' unpaid parental leave in the period up to the child becoming five (if the child is disabled this leave can be taken up to the age of 18). No more than four weeks can be taken in any one year. The purpose of the leave must be to care for the child and it must be taken in blocks of at least a week. The employee must also give you 21 days' notice of wishing to take time off. If you wish the individual to postpone their leave for a valid business reason you may do so (except at the time of birth or adoption) provided you do so within seven days of their request and allow them to take the leave within six months of their original request. In other words, it's a postponement – not a refusal.

One final area that can occasionally crop up is where a woman returning to work is breastfeeding. It may be that the child is in childcare nearby or the mother wishes to express milk for a later time. In this case, discussion with the individual is always the preferred solution, but as far as the law is concerned you should undertake a health and safety risk assessment (as with pregnancy), and consider factors such as where a new mother could breastfeed in clean conditions, or express milk privately and store it hygienically. While there are no rights to specific 'time off', you do have a general duty not to discriminate against someone on the grounds of pregnancy or childbirth.

Although all these rights might appear to provide extensive time off, it has to be said that currently only maternity leave is widely used. Many employees prefer to book holidays at the time of a birth – since they are paid in full – rather than take paternity leave, and at the time of writing it is the exception rather than the rule to receive a request for shared parental leave, although take-up is anticipated to increase over time.

CHAPTER 11:

# On the rocks

At some point when you employ people, you'll come up against a situation where one or more of your staff breaks a rule, behaves in an unacceptable way or does something in a negligent way. As a manager, you need to make the employee aware of this and make sure that the behaviour is not repeated.

The fact that this is generally known as 'discipline' harks back to the days when it did imply some form of punishment – and when the accepted form of management was based on military lines. Theory X management (which we described in Chapter 7) is its modern descendant.

Most issues that arise can be resolved informally – the purpose being to let the employee know what they've done wrong and what they need to do to resolve the situation. In some cases, however, this may not solve the problem and more formal action may need to be taken, or the issue that occurs is of a more serious nature and you don't think that informal action is sufficient.

For many managers, putting matters into a formal disciplinary situation is seen as nerve-wracking and confrontational. However, not following the process when it's needed can actually make matters worse, since the individual can – legitimately – claim that they were not aware of how serious you considered things to be.

Before you take any action, you need to be sure that the employee is aware of the rules. It is very difficult to take any action against someone who doesn't know that what they've done (or not done) is wrong. That's why a good induction process for new employees, and clear and easily accessible rules and procedures, are so important (see Chapter 5).

If you do need to take formal action, then you need to follow a number of basic principles to make sure that you do things fairly – this becomes especially important if you think that dismissing the employee (see Chapter 13) is a possible consequence. Even at the early stages however, the way in which you treat a disciplinary issue will send out a message to your staff about whether you are a fair and reasonable employer – and given the two-way nature of the employment relationship this can have an impact in many ways.

The first principle is that you need to take action promptly. Raising issues weeks or months after they've occurred is not acceptable – apart from the fact that memories of what actually happened may have faded, an employee whose behaviour is not challenged in some way at the time can justifiably think that you consider it acceptable.

Secondly, you must not pre-judge the issue – you should investigate the facts and give the employee a chance to put their side of the story before reaching a decision. Investigation does not mean that you have to play Sherlock Holmes – it simply means gathering the facts surrounding the issue. So, if you have an employee who is frequently late, it could be as simple as getting a print out of their clocking in times as evidence. If the issue is more complex, you may need to carry out a more detailed investigation. In some cases (again particularly where dismissal is a possibility) it may be better to ask another manager, or an independent person (for example your accountant or an HR consultant), to carry out the investigation, if you have the resources to be able to do this.

Thirdly, you should hold a formal meeting to discuss the matter, before which the employee is informed of the issue you intend to raise (and given any investigation information). Employees have the right to be accompanied at any such disciplinary hearing, either by a fellow employee or an official of a trade union. Trade Union officials (of whom more in Chapter 17) are the only people outside your organisation who have a right to attend – an employee cannot bring their partner, their mum, or their best friend unless those individuals also work for you. Nor can they bring in a solicitor or other external legal adviser.

There is one 'good practice' exception to this. If you need to discipline a disabled employee who requires some form of assistance (e.g. a support worker to read documents, or a sign language interpreter), then you should allow such individuals to attend, even if they're not employed by you. This would count as a reasonable adjustment under the Equality Act.

While the employee has the right to be accompanied, it's also worth mentioning that you may be accompanied – this might simply by having an independent notetaker, or you may want to use a professional adviser (especially if dismissal is a possible consequence).

It's important to remember that in an employment situation, you don't need to have cast-iron proof of the issue one way or another. You simply need 'reasonable grounds' for making your decision. So, if it's a case of one person's word against another, you need to decide who you believe – known as the 'balance of probability'.

Finally, if you do take some disciplinary action, like issuing a warning, then the employee should be given the right to appeal, which should normally be heard by another manager – usually someone more senior than whoever made the original decision. In a small organisation this isn't always possible (in fact, if you're the owner-manager there's no-one higher than you) and so you need to allow the individual the right to ask you to review your decision.

An appeal (or review) is not a rehearing of the original disciplinary issue – it's an opportunity for the individual to raise points, if they think that the decision is too harsh given the circumstances, or that you have behaved inconsistently (for example, giving them a final warning when you have given a warning to others in the past for similar errors). The only occasion where an appeal might become a rehearing would be if the original disciplinary meeting was so flawed that it couldn't be considered fair (for example, if the individual was not presented with the investigation, or not allowed to state their case) or if significant new evidence that wasn't available at the original hearing came to light. Employees have the same right to be accompanied at an appeal as they do for the disciplinary meeting.

All disciplinary decisions should be confirmed in writing, as should the outcomes of any appeals. You also need to decide how long any warning will stay on someone's record – six or 12 months is the norm, although you may be able to justify longer in certain circumstances. What you can't do is keep a warning on record indefinitely.

It's important that whatever sanction you impose – a warning or final warning – you also make clear what improvements you require the employee to make (and what support, if necessary, you can give them to achieve this). For example, if someone has dealt poorly with a customer which has led to a complaint, then you need to make them aware of the procedures they should be following and, if appropriate, provide training for them.

## Breaking point

If the person doesn't improve, and either repeats the problem or breaches another company rule or procedure, you can escalate the process. Many older disciplinary processes had a 'verbal' warning, followed by a 'written' warning, followed by a 'final written' warning and then dismissal. It's not necessary to have all these stages – in fact, since it's important to confirm all disciplinary action in writing, the concept of a 'verbal' warning is redundant. But, if you do wish to have two stages before issuing a final warning then it's better to refer to them as stage one and stage two warnings. For a small organisation it's perfectly OK to have simply a warning, final warning and then dismissal.

If an employee is on a final warning, then any form of disciplinary sanction after this can (and, in most cases, should) trigger a dismissal. It's akin to a football situation, where a second yellow card offence will automatically result in a red card (a sending off) – regardless of what the actual second offence is. We'll look more at handling dismissal in the later chapters on Ending the Employment Relationship (see Chapter 13).

The disciplinary process looks at how to deal with an employee who's let you down in some way. But, just as important, is the way in which you, as an employer, respond to and deal with situations where your employees feel that you have behaved inconsistently, or below the standards that you have set for yourself. This is known as the grievance procedure.

As with disciplinary situations, it's always helpful to try and resolve employee concerns informally. But if it isn't possible, then you need to meet formally with the employee to discuss their issue – as with a disciplinary situation, the employee has the right to be accompanied and you can request that the grievance is put to you in writing. The same principles of dealing with matters promptly, ensuring that issues are investigated properly if required, giving your response in writing and allowing a right of appeal also apply.

A typical grievance situation is where the employee believes your organisation's rules have been misinterpreted or applied inconsistently. For example, if you have a rule that no employee can take more than two weeks' holiday at any one time, but you allow Bill to take three weeks and then turn down a similar request from Sally, she would have grounds for a grievance. Similarly, if an employee wants to complain about the behaviour of a manager or other member of staff (for example, a suggestion that they're behaving in an aggressive or bullying manner) they can use the grievance procedure. The grievance procedure is not for personal moans however – nor is it a forum for challenging your company rules or procedures (in the above example, provided you applied the rule consistently, Sally could not raise a grievance about the fact that you do not allow more than two weeks' leave).

In many cases, the individual employee will be challenging a decision you've made. It's important (though understandably difficult) that you don't allow personal feelings to get involved in this process. There's no need to be defensive if you genuinely believe that you made the correct decision. If you're not the most senior manager in a business, or if you have a board of directors or trustees you report to, it may reach the point where the process goes above your level and your decision is overturned. In that case, the person making that decision should explain to you – outside the process – why they made their decision and what you need to learn from it.

As an employer, you have a particular responsibility to avoid your employees being harassed or bullied – particularly if this is as a consequence of them having a protected characteristic (sex, race, etc). It's important to be clear what you, as an employer, consider to be unacceptable behaviour (for example, in some organisations casual swearing – what used to be called 'industrial language' – is accepted, while in others it is not tolerated). There is, of course, plenty of behaviour which isn't acceptable in any circumstances – violence, inappropriate sexual comments etc. Bullying is really a 'specialised' form of harassment – it describes the situation where a manager or supervisor uses their authority over a member of staff to be overly critical or controlling. The important thing is that, if a member of staff raises an issue of potential harassment or bullying, you deal with it promptly and effectively.

Again, if matters can be resolved informally, this is always the best approach. Sometimes another member of staff may not be aware that their behaviour is unwelcome or causing distress. But, whatever the situation, you need to treat it seriously and consider it under the grievance or disciplinary process, as appropriate.

Sometimes, you may find that starting a disciplinary process against an employee leads to that employee raising a 'counter'-grievance, either against you or another member of staff. In such a situation, you might want to suspend the disciplinary process while the grievance is dealt with, or if the two issues are closely intertwined you may deal with them concurrently.

There is one further unusual type of grievance, which gives the employee particular legal protection. This is most commonly known as 'whistleblowing', although it's more properly known as making a 'public interest disclosure'. It describes situations where the employee believes they have discovered illegal activity being carried out either by the organisation or its employees or directors (or trustees, in the case of charities) – this illegal activity can include breaches of health and safety or environmental damage, as well as issues like bribery or criminal offences. Provided the employee makes the allegations in good faith – in other words they reasonably believe them to be true, even if they subsequently turn out not to be – they're given protection against dismissal or victimisation by their employer.

If an employee raises a whistleblowing issue with you then it's essential you treat it both seriously and as confidentially as possible. If you don't (or if the employee doesn't feel able to raise matters with you because they think you are implicated) the employee is perfectly entitled to go to other 'prescribed people', like a regulatory body (e.g. the Charity Commission, Office of Fair Trading), HMRC (for example if it is a matter related to tax evasion) or the police. Employees do not get protection if, for example, they go to the press before raising matters either with you or a prescribed organisation.

Whistleblowing is a rare occurrence in a small organisation, and can be dealt with through a similar approach to the grievance procedure, though some organisations may want to set up specific arrangements (for example, many charities nominate one of their trustees to be the point of contact in such situations).

# PART 3

# D.I.V.O.R.C.E

CHAPTER 12:

# I'm leaving...

Just like a marriage, either side can end the employment relationship, although – unlike a marriage – there normally needs to be a period of notice before the relationship ends. The circumstances where no notice is needed are outlined later.

If the end of the relationship is amicable, then there's no reason why it should cause an employer any difficulties at all. Things become difficult when one side (most frequently the employee) does not want things to end, and these are the sort of situations that can end in the work equivalent of the divorce court – the Employment Tribunal.

In this chapter we will look at how the employee can finish the relationship – in the next two we will examine how you as the employer can end it.

An employee can end the relationship with you in one of the following ways:

- By resigning with notice;
- By resigning without notice – often, but not always, the start of a constructive dismissal claim;
- By retiring – this is in effect the same as resignation;
- By dying;
- By being unable to fulfil the contract for some external reason – known in legal jargon as 'frustration'. The most common example of this would be if an employee were jailed for a criminal offence, although technically a long-term illness which prevented the employee from working could be classed as frustration.

In your contract of employment, you should have specified a period of notice that an employee must give to end it. Typically, this is a month, although it can be as little as a week and can be as much as six months for senior roles.

## Resigning with notice

If one of your employees resigns – which can be done verbally or in writing – then you have three options, depending on how your working relationship has been.

If they do resign verbally, then it's always sensible to ask them to confirm it in writing, or write back to them to acknowledge their resignation. As we've noted in earlier chapters, email is a valid form of written communication.

Your options are:

- Have the individual work their notice period;
- Not require the individual to work their notice period, but keep them as an employee on the books (known as 'garden leave');
- Waive your right to notice and terminate their employment immediately.

If the individual is an employee you want to keep, you may well want to discuss with them the reasons for their resignation, to see if there's anything you can do to get them to withdraw it. It may be that the person is dissatisfied with their pay, or frustrated by lack of promotion opportunities, and you may be able to persuade them to stay. However, you can't force them to discuss these matters and if the employee is adamant that they want to go, there's nothing you can do to prevent them leaving you. Depending on your day-to-day working relationship, you will often be aware if someone is dissatisfied with their current situation and you may already know whether there's anything you can do to resolve it (especially if you've used some of the management techniques described in previous chapters).

It is always sensible to keep matters amicable, even if you're losing someone important to your business. The key thing is, having accepted the resignation, to agree with them a proper 'handover' of any work they are currently doing. It's human nature that, during notice, individuals will often switch off or do the bare minimum, no matter how professional and committed they have been previously. Mentally, they've already left your employment, even if physically they are still there.

There may, of course, be situations where you don't want the person around work. This might be because they're in a role which could cause significant disruption, or where they would have access to business information that you no longer want them to have. It's not uncommon for IT specialists (who could cause damage to your computer systems) or sales people – who have details of and access to key customers – to be asked to leave work immediately. However, in order to prevent these individuals from going straight to a potential competitor, they are often placed on garden leave – in other words, during their notice period they continue to receive their pay and other benefits, but are not required to attend work and are prevented from accessing company information.

The other scenario is where you have an employee who, either because of their performance or attitude, is someone you don't want in the business. In this case, you can, on receipt of their resignation, waive your right to notice and terminate their employment immediately. In the case of someone with a long notice period of, say three months, you may decide that you only want them to work for a shorter period.

## Resigning without notice

Sometimes, an employee may resign and leave immediately, or fail to give the correct notice – they may only work a week when they are required to give a month's notice, for example. This can create a problem for you, especially if the individual works in a key role or you'll find it difficult to recruit a replacement.

Legally, you can sue an ex-employee who resigns without giving their contractual notice. To succeed, though, you will have to be able to demonstrate some financial loss to the business, and you will, of course, incur legal fees. You also need to consider whether the individual could pay you back even if you won. For this reason, in 99% of cases employers have to accept the situation, however reluctantly.

A far more serious situation is when an employee resigns and commences a claim for constructive dismissal. 'Constructive dismissal' is a phrase that strikes terror into the hearts of many employers, primarily because they don't clearly understand what it actually means.

As we discussed right at the start, the cornerstone of any employment relationship is trust and confidence between the two parties. Essentially, constructive dismissal is a situation where you, as the employer, behave in such a way that the employee can no longer have any trust and confidence in you.

In the next chapter we'll examine the sort of things that an employee might do to destroy your trust and confidence in them, but they are, in the main, very serious matters (criminal activities, defrauding the company, fighting, endangering people by ignoring health and safety rules). Equally, for an employee to claim that your actions breach trust and confidence, you must have done something very serious – for example, demoting somebody without notice, bullying or harassing them (or allowing others to bully or harass them), failing to pay them, or making unfounded accusations against them which might damage their professional reputation.

To succeed in a claim, the individual must resign immediately (or very shortly) after the alleged action has taken place. They must then demonstrate to an Employment Tribunal that your actions were so serious that they could consider themselves to have been dismissed. Even if they convince the tribunal of this, they must still show that the dismissal was unfair under the normal unfair dismissal rules (which you'll see in the next chapter). Finally, if they do all this, they will still only gain the same compensation that a person is entitled to for unfair dismissal – there is no additional penalty for the fact it is 'constructive'.

Facing a claim for constructive dismissal (or any kind of unfair dismissal) is never a pleasant experience, but you can be reassured that it's actually far less frequent than popular employment myth suggests, and is far harder for an employee to win their case.

## Retirement

Since the abolition of the default retirement age in early 2011, it is no longer possible for an employer to force someone to retire at a particular age (65 being the most common previously), unless you can 'objectively justify' it – in other words, demonstrate some solid business reason (or legal restriction) why you need to enforce it. For example, if you are operating in a safety-critical environment and can show that performance falls significantly after a certain age (air traffic controllers are cited as the most common example), then you can justify retirement at a specified age.

The majority of businesses won't be able to use this justification however, and so employees have the right to continue to work as long as they wish. If they decide that they want to retire, all they have to do is resign with notice in the way described above. If you want to get rid of them, then you must dismiss them in the same way as you would any other employee, which we'll discuss in the next chapter. Not dealing with issues with an older worker because 'they're retiring soon' is no longer an option.

## Dying

Although it's rare, especially in a small organisation, there are occasions when one of your employees may die. This is obviously a very traumatic experience for the individual's family, but also has major repercussions for you and your other employees. How you deal with the situation as an employer may well reflect on how you are perceived by your staff, customers and other key contacts.

If the individual dies outside work (perhaps after a long illness, or unexpectedly – for example, as a result of a traffic accident) then you need to think about how you will communicate the message to their colleagues and also any outside contacts they may have dealt with (like customers and suppliers). You'll need to be supportive of anyone who is particularly distressed as a result of the news (for example, someone who worked particularly closely with the individual) and you should be very sympathetic to any requests for time off to attend the funeral. Even if you didn't know the individual particularly well, it is good practice for someone senior to attend the funeral as a representative of the organisation as well as sending a letter of condolence on hearing the news.

It is always important to maintain contact with the next of kin, provided you do this sensitively, and it may be helpful for one person to act as a point of contact so the family are not having to deal with enquiries from work colleagues.

There are several 'practical' things that you have to do as an employer. Firstly, you will need to ensure that you advise your payroll provider so that any final payments due can be calculated – you may not be able to pay them immediately as you will not normally be able to access the individual's bank account and may require letters of administration to be able to release the money. You also need to issue the normal 'leaver' documents (a P45, etc.) and, if you have a pension scheme you will need to advise the administrators. This is particularly important as many pension schemes have 'death benefits' which can be paid out immediately and are an important support for the family.

It sometimes occurs that an individual has been 'overpaid' – if, for example, you pay monthly and the individual dies mid-month. While legally you may seek to reclaim this overpayment, the overwhelming majority of employers will simply write this off.

Every situation is different, and the best advice is to be guided by the family or next of kin.

If an individual dies in work, then in addition to the above steps, you must first of all contact the emergency services – and do not move the body – and then contact the Health and Safety Executive (HSE). If the death is as a result of an accident at work, the HSE will conduct a full investigation and, depending on their findings, you may be prosecuted. Depending on how responsible the courts find you, you may be imprisoned, or your organisation receive a heavy fine. If an employee dies within 12 months of, and as a result of, an accident at work, the HSE will also investigate, with the same potential consequences.

Regardless of the circumstances, you also need to consider how you will support any colleagues who were working with the employee at the time, or who found the body. You may also receive enquiries from the media and need to consider how you respond.

If nothing else, the death of an employee brings home one of the key points of this book – that you are dealing with another person and it is your relationship with them that is at the heart of successful people management.

## 'Frustration of Contract'

This is a legal concept, which describes a situation where an employee is unable to carry out their duties due to some external factor preventing them. For example, if an employee was imprisoned for a significant period they would clearly be unable to work for you. Equally someone who is sick for a long period and unable to attend work could be considered to have frustrated their contract. A third situation might occur when an employee simply 'disappears' – fails to attend work without any explanation, does not respond to any attempts to contact them and you later find has moved away.

Frustration can become quite complex and in many cases it is easier (and legally safer) for you as the employer to take a more active approach and dismiss the individual. We'll discuss this in the next chapter.

CHAPTER 13:

# Unreasonable behaviour

Situations or circumstances sometimes arise where you want to end your relationship with an employee.

Other than when a contract has a defined end (either a 'temporary' or 'fixed term' contract) – as the employer, you can only end it for one of the following reasons:

- Capability (the person's ability to do the job);
- Conduct (the person's behaviour);
- Legal restriction (some other aspect of law prevents you continuing to employ them);
- Redundancy (you're ceasing to carry out the work the person undertakes);
- Some other 'substantial reason' – a legal term that we'll describe later.

These five reasons are known as the 'fair reasons' for dismissal.

If you dismiss someone for any other reason, then this becomes an unfair dismissal and they have grounds for an employment tribunal claim. Some situations are known as 'automatically unfair' – in other words, if you dismiss someone for them, there's no possible defence. These include any form of discrimination (if you dismissed someone because of their race etc); as a consequence of pregnancy or maternity; for being a member of, or seeking to join a trade union; for reporting health and safety concerns; or for trying to use one of the basic employment rights that individuals have (like asking to be accompanied at a disciplinary or grievance hearing, or requesting that you provide them with a contract).

However, the majority of unfair dismissal claims revolve around not the reason for dismissal, but the way in which it was conducted. To successfully defend against a claim, you need to establish not only a fair reason but also a fair process. We'll look at this in more detail later in the chapter.

With only one exception, dismissal is always with notice – so if you sack somebody and their contract states that you have to give them one month's notice, then either they remain working for that month, or, more commonly, are either paid in lieu of notice (given one months' salary but their employment ends immediately) or put on garden leave (see the previous chapter) for the month. One peculiarity is that the law lays down minimum periods of notice that you, as the employer, must give – but does not specify any that an employee has to give (which is why it's important to include it in the contract). This statutory notice period is one week for the first two years of employment, then a week for each complete year, up to a maximum of 12. An employee is entitled to the longer of contractual notice or statutory notice (so an employee whose contract says one months' notice who has worked for you for two years is entitled to one month; an employee with an identical contract who has worked for you for six years is entitled to six weeks' notice).

At any meeting where you're considering dismissal, the individual has the right to be accompanied, as outlined in earlier chapters, by a work colleague or trade union official.

Employees who are dismissed have the right to appeal against the decision. This should normally be heard by a senior individual who has not been involved in the decision

As handling redundancies has a particular set of legal rules and procedures to follow, we'll cover this in the next chapter.

## Capability

This covers two distinct areas within an employment situation – where an individual can't do the job despite every effort to support them to do it, and also the situation where a person is off on long-term sickness.

When an individual's performance is not up to standard, you need to ensure you've gone through the formal process outlined in the performance management chapters to be able to demonstrate that you have given the person every opportunity to improve, and that you have provided the necessary support. You'll also need to show that you've made the employee aware that a failure to improve could result in their dismissal. For this reason, many employers use their disciplinary procedure to ensure that the employee is fully aware of the consequences of the process. However, as long as you can demonstrate that you have followed a proper procedure, given the individual the right to be accompanied at the dismissal, and the right to appeal, you should be able to defend a decision to dismiss.

Long-term sickness is a more difficult scenario, especially as you'll need to take care that you are not falling foul of any potential disability issues. Even without that, however, you need to balance the fact that the individual has a serious illness against your requirement to have an employee in post.

First of all, as we discussed in the handling absence chapter, you need to decide when someone's absence through illness is causing you serious operational problems. To reiterate, there is no fixed definition of what is a 'long term' illness – a small organisation could consider this to be after four to six weeks – a larger organisation may be able to manage for longer.

To recap the process we outlined in the earlier chapter, you need to:

Go and see the person if they are well enough – in part to find out if there's anything you can do for them, but also to obtain their consent to get in touch with their GP or specialist for a medical report on their condition. This report is solely to determine whether or not the individual is likely to return to work, and if they are able to return whether there are any conditions or advice the doctor can give you. If they don't wish to receive a home visit, then write to them along the same lines.

Assuming they give consent to a doctor's report, write to their doctor enclosing the individual's consent form. Remember that doctors typically take three to four weeks to reply.

Depending on what the report says, you need to consider all the options open to you – including dismissal - and consult with the individual.

If the employee doesn't consent to a doctor's report, you do have the right to take decisions without medical advice. However, you would be well advised to consult with them again – and if possible get them to change their decision – before taking any decisions on their future employment. In this consultation, stress to them that you would prefer to take action based on the fullest information about their condition possible, but that you will do so without medical advice if necessary.

If all other options have proved not possible, and the individual has still not returned to work by a deadline (which you have informed them of), then you may dismiss with notice, allowing an appeal.

Having to dismiss someone who is ill is never pleasant and you should not take this step lightly. But, in the end, you have to balance the individual's personal circumstances with the effect that their absence is having on your business or organisation.

## Conduct

The process for conduct was outlined in the chapter on discipline and grievances. In a case of cumulative misconduct, an individual may have a final warning on their record and then commit a further act of misconduct. At this stage, you would convene a disciplinary hearing and make them aware in any correspondence that their dismissal is a potential outcome.

Carry out the disciplinary hearing as you would normally, ensuring that the employee has the right to be accompanied and to put forward their case before any decision is reached.

It's actually quite unusual to go through the full disciplinary process for a conduct dismissal. The majority of conduct-related dismissals are as a result of a single act which leads to summary dismissal. This is known as 'gross misconduct' – and is where the employee's actions or behaviour are such that all trust and confidence is destroyed. Clearly, something which creates this belief must be very serious, and the most commonly cited examples are things such as theft, fraud or physical assault – actions which seriously affect health and safety, or negligence which seriously damages the service or reputation of the organisation.

Because gross misconduct leads to dismissal without notice, it is sometimes incorrectly referred to as 'instant dismissal'. However, you must still carry out a proper disciplinary investigation and hold a full hearing before coming to a decision. If you don't want the individual around the premises while you investigate matters, you can (and, in most cases, should) suspend them while you do this – it is important to be clear to them that the suspension is on full pay and that it is a preliminary measure, not a disciplinary sanction.

## Legal restriction

This is a fairly unusual occurrence in most organisations, but arises where something – possibly outside work – prevents your employee from doing their job. The most obvious example is where an employee is required to drive for their role and loses their licence.

In this situation, before dismissing you should look at whether you can accommodate the employee on non-driving work, but if this isn't possible then you should dismiss in the normal way – advise them that you are contemplating dismissal, allow them to be accompanied at any hearing, give appropriate notice and allow an appeal.

## Some other 'substantial reason'

This is a great legal phrase – essentially it means 'something you can't fit into one of the other categories'. The key word here though is 'substantial' – it must be something that either breaks the trust and confidence you have in the employee, or where you have a valid business reason which is not related to a reduction in staffing.

It's probably best illustrated by a number of examples.

One situation that you can often encounter in a small organisation is where a key member of your management team has a fundamentally different view from you or your board about the correct strategy for the future and, as a consequence, may become uncooperative. If their attitude continues, you may come to the view that you no longer want them in the organisation.

There are no issues about their capability to do the job, nor is their behaviour sufficient to merit misconduct, but you'd be able to justify ending the relationship under 'some other substantial reason' if you could show that their attitude was having a serious effect on your organisation.

Another case of where dismissal can be justified for 'some other substantial reason' is where you need to end the contract of a temporary maternity leave cover. Again, there are no issues of capability or conduct, it's simply the case that the person they're providing cover for is due to return.

A third example is a business reorganisation, which doesn't involve redundancies, but may require different roles which existing staff are unqualified for. This is covered more fully in the next chapter on redundancy.

## Fixed term employees

At the start of this chapter, we pointed out that the ending of a fixed term contract was a case where the need to justify dismissal with one of the five valid reasons didn't apply. But it is important to remember that employees on fixed term contracts have a number of rights, and these must be adhered to.

Essentially, someone employed under a fixed term contract is entitled to receive equal treatment to someone employed under a 'permanent' contract. So:

- If they have more than two years' service they're entitled to a redundancy payment and have the right to make a claim for unfair dismissal;

- They must receive the same conditions of service as a 'permanent' employee with the same service (e.g. if someone can join a pension scheme after three months, the fixed term employee must also be allowed to);

- At the end of a fixed term contract the employee must be treated as a 'redundant' employee would be, so he or she should be considered for any other suitable vacancies in the company;

- In a redundancy situation, a fixed term worker cannot automatically be selected ahead of a permanent employee – fair selection criteria must still be used.

A fixed term employee would also be able to claim for breach of contract if their contract was terminated early (and if successful, be paid the balance of their contract).

CHAPTER 14:

# It's not you, it's me ...

At some point, almost every organisation is faced with a situation where it needs to reduce the number of staff it employs. This could be because demand has dropped; because new technology means that the same product or service can be done by fewer people; because the organisation wishes to move out of one market into another; or because it wishes to relocate.

If one of these circumstances arises, you're faced with a potential redundancy situation. Redundancy is – like the four reasons discussed in the previous chapter – a fair reason for dismissing an employee. The big difference is that it's not as a consequence of the individual employee's behaviour or ability; it is as result of an organisational change. The individual has nothing to do with the decision and it's not uncommon for a company to lose some of its best-qualified staff in such a situation.

As a dismissal, it is subject to the normal unfair dismissal rules, so it's important not only to be sure that it is a redundancy, but also that you get the procedure correct.

So what is exactly is redundancy? While I have deliberately avoided quoting the law in most of this book, the definition of redundancy in the Employment Rights Act is quite clear and is worth reading:

'... an employee ... shall be taken to be dismissed by reason of redundancy if the dismissal is attributable wholly or mainly to:

a) the fact that his employer has ceased, or intends to cease, to carry on the business for the purposes of which the employee was employed by him, or has ceased, or intends to cease, to carry on that business in the place where the employee was employed or;

b) the fact that the requirements of that business for employees to carry out work of a particular kind, or for employees to carry out work of a particular kind in the place where he was so employed, have ceased or diminished or are expected to cease or diminish.'

In other words, part (a) describes the situation where either a company is closing down completely, or is closing down a particular factory or location, while situation (b) is the case where an employer requires fewer people (either overall or in one particular location), for example due to a downturn in business. While both types of redundancy occur regularly, situation (b) is probably the more common in smaller organisations.

Before we move further, it's also useful to make clear what is not a redundancy situation. If you are simply reorganising work but still require the same number of staff (albeit doing different jobs) then this is not redundancy. For example, if you employ four accounts staff, you may think the same work could be done more efficiently by having two accountants with more responsibility and two administrators with less. The existing staff could all potentially be redeployed into one or other of the new roles. You may however be able to say that this is dismissal for 'some other substantial reason' if you did need to dismiss any of the existing staff (for example if they lacked a necessary qualification) as a result of the reorganisation. In the example above, if you needed the two accountants in the reorganised team to hold a recognised accountancy qualification and none of the current four staff held such a qualification – and had no prospect of achieving it within a reasonable timescale – this might apply.

If a redundancy situation does occur, then as the employer you have a number of distinct tasks to undertake:

- You must consult with affected individuals prior to making a final decision, in a meaningful way and with a view to avoiding redundancy if possible;

- You must consult collectively with staff, and depending on the number of redundancies you may be required to notify the appropriate government department (currently the Department of Business, Energy and Industrial Strategy) before anyone is actually dismissed;

- You may have to pay anyone made redundant a statutory redundancy payment. This amount – which is laid down by the Government and depends on age and length of service – is tax-free (currently up to £30,000) and is on top of any notice period or pay in lieu of notice.

## The human costs

Before we begin to discuss the process in detail, it's worthwhile reminding yourself that the consequences of redundancy can be serious, not only for the individuals losing their jobs but also the colleagues that remain, and the business overall.

Redundancy is a factor over which most staff have no control and the people who are made redundant are leaving generally through no fault of their own.

It's important therefore to plan for how you are going to deal with the emotional consequences as well as the legal consequences. Even if staff are aware that business is not good, that rarely prepares them fully for the shock of being told that they might be made redundant. You will need to anticipate tears, aggression, disbelief and other emotional responses – and decide how you will react to them. It's often better to give affected staff the remainder of the day off when you tell them, or even a couple of days, so that they have time to think about things and discuss the situation with family, advisers etc. (They are hardly likely to be particularly productive if they remain in work, quite apart from any disruption or poor morale they may cause).

For this reason, it's also sensible not to announce redundancies on a Friday – because the individuals affected will be left with a whole weekend where they can do nothing but reflect on their situation.

You'll also be under scrutiny from staff members who aren't directly affected. How professionally and compassionately you treat redundant individuals will be noticed by their colleagues, who – if they see their friends and co-workers being treated poorly – may decide that their own loyalty to the organisation is reduced. This will result in reduced motivation and productivity, probably just at a time your organisation needs good performance most.

Finally, don't underestimate the emotional effect on you and your managerial colleagues who have to handle the situation. It's never ever a pleasant business and you may well feel a mixture of guilt and upset at the circumstances – particularly if the individuals are people you know well or who have worked for you for a long time. As hard as it may seem, you cannot worry about how Bill is going to pay his mortgage, or how Sally will explain to her children that she doesn't work anymore. That doesn't mean that you should be uncaring or unsympathetic, but your objective has to be ensuring that the organisation will survive.

Redundancy is not an easy option for an organisation looking to reduce its costs. In fact, this is a situation where your legal obligations (to avoid redundancies where possible) coincide with what might be regarded as ethical concerns – given the emotional consequences, redundancies should always be the last resort for any company or organisation.

## Individual consultation

Once you've made a business decision to make redundancies, you must notify the affected staff as soon as possible. This is not making them redundant at this stage, but is putting them 'at risk' of redundancy. For example, if you employ ten staff in a call centre and decide that you only need six, then all ten must be put at risk, even though only four of them are likely to lose their job. Alternatively, if you've decided that you no longer need to employ your quality assurance team of four people, all of them are at risk.

Having put affected staff at risk, you need to consult with the individuals and make a genuine attempt to avoid having to make someone redundant. So, you need to consider any suggestions that the affected staff members may make. These might be that the savings you need can be achieved in a different way; whether or not there is any scope to work fewer hours, or whether the work can be reorganised differently to save their particular job. Of course, none of these options may be viable, but you must consider them and if you reject them you need to explain your reasons why.

You also need to consider whether there are any other jobs in the organisation that the person could be redeployed to. There are three important things to think about here. Firstly, you do not have to 'create' a new job, nor are you required to employ someone who is completely unsuited to the job that is available.

Secondly, you must make someone who is at risk aware of all possible vacancies (including in other locations) so that they can take the decision as to whether or not they want to be considered (even if you think they would not want them). As a practical example of this, I was once involved in making the manager of a bus garage redundant. The company always had vacancies for bus drivers, but this wasn't mentioned to him during consultation, as it was assumed that he wouldn't want to take the pay cut and he would also find it difficult to go back to the shop floor and work with people he had previously managed. At his appeal hearing, he successfully argued that he would have taken a driver's job if it had been offered to him, as he still held his PCV licence and, as he had only 12 months to go before he could apply for early retirement, continuing in work would protect his pension benefits.

Thirdly, you need to consider how you will fill the vacancy. If the individual already possesses many of the skills (but not necessarily all of them) then you may want to redeploy them straight in to the new role and agree a training plan to give them the missing skills.

If they don't have all the skills, or if there are several people interested in the role, you may want to restrict the advert to internal candidates or just those who are at risk. If they don't appear to have any, or very few, of the skills required, then you can legitimately continue with any external recruitment process but advise them that they can apply if they wish.

If you do redeploy a member of staff, both you and they have a month's trial period, during which time their right to a redundancy payment is protected. So if the individual doesn't like the job, or you think they are not really up to it, then they won't lose their redundancy payment for trying a new role.

Sometimes an individual will move into a role on a lower salary. In this situation, once the trial period has passed, they will be employed on the terms and conditions of the new role. You are under no obligation to 'protect' salary beyond this initial trial, although you can if you wish. If you do decide to protect salary, this should be for a time limited period as indefinite protection might lead you to an Equal Pay claim (see later chapter 15).

## Selection for redundancy

We talked before about the situation where you have ten staff doing the same job and you only require six. The key question is – how do you choose the four staff to be made redundant?

In this situation you have two options. You can either ask all ten to reapply for their own jobs and select the best six on interview, or you can use some form of selection criteria.

Using application and interview is not always the best way in this situation. Firstly, it can be extremely demotivating for an individual to be asked to apply for their own job (even if they are subsequently successful). Secondly, there's a danger that the candidates who impress at interview are not necessarily the ones you want to retain – but it is very difficult to justify making someone redundant if they have performed well at the interview (and would almost certainly give them grounds for an unfair dismissal claim).

Selection criteria are preferable, but you need to ensure that they are fair and non-discriminatory. In the past, 'last in, first out' was commonly used, but today you can't use service as the only criterion for the reason that it is potentially age discriminatory (since older workers are likely to be longer serving and therefore young workers are disadvantaged solely because of their age).

That's not to say that service can't be used at all, but it must be coupled with other factors. These selection criteria can include a mixture of objective factors (such as sickness record, disciplinary record, qualifications) and subjective ones (such as an assessment of work performance, attitude). Wherever possible, you should have evidence to support subjective criteria, for example through an appraisal or performance review process. If such things don't exist then, if you can, use two or more managers who know the individual well to assess their performance (that way you can minimise arguments that 'my boss has always disliked me').

The criteria you intend to use are subject to consultation, both with the individuals and during any collective consultation process. That doesn't mean that you have to change them to suit particular individuals (in fact you should avoid as much as you can any suggestion that they are biased for or against specific people). But if there is a strong view that something should be changed then you should consider changing it. For example, in one recent case I dealt with the company planned to use lateness as a factor. Staff were unhappy that this was included because the company had a culture of people working beyond the end of the day, and they felt that those who came in 'late' but made up the time would be penalised. The company agreed to amend the criterion.

Once you've completed the selection process, you must ensure that you consult again to allow the individuals the opportunity to query any aspects of their score (for example, if you have used service, have you got their start date right?). The affected employee may also want to query their performance scores, but needs to come up with evidence as to why the score should be different, rather than simply the fact they disagree with it.

Finally, before announcing the decision, check your arithmetic is correct! There is nothing worse than telling individual A that they are redundant and B that they are safe, then finding that you've added up incorrectly and the result is the other way round.

## Interviewing

Although interviewing's not the best way for the situation described above, there may be situations where you want to use it. For example, you may be merging two regions and want to appoint one overall manager, who has significant extra responsibilities, from the two existing regional managers. Here interviewing might be the best solution, allowing you to pick the best candidate for the future regardless of previous performance, service etc. Obviously you need to ensure that the interviewing process is done correctly, as outlined in the recruitment chapter, to avoid any suggestion that the process is a sham.

## No selection needed

Sometimes there will be no need to select – you may be getting rid of an individual, unique post, closing down a whole team or even an entire business. In this situation you simply need to look at ways to avoid redundancy, as described in the individual consultation process above.

## Collective consultation

If you are planning to make redundancies, you may well need to consult with staff on a collective basis. If you're planning more than 20 in any one location, you must consult with staff collectively.

Where an organisation recognises trade unions, collective consultation is normally done with union officials – often through already established consultation or negotiation procedures. If you don't have unions, then staff need to select representatives to meet with you to discuss matters.

You must provide the representatives with the following information, in writing:

· the reasons for redundancies;

· the numbers and categories of employees involved;

· the numbers of employees in these categories employed at the establishment;

· how you plan to select employees for redundancy;

· how you will carry out redundancies;

· how you will work out redundancy payments.

As with individual consultation, you must listen to any comments that the representatives make and, if necessary, change or amend your proposals accordingly.

Consultation must begin 30 days before you give the first redundancy notice if you are making between 20 and 99 staff redundant, and must begin 45 days before you give anyone notice if planning to make more than 100 people redundant.

(One of the many employment myths is that you must give '90 days' notice of redundancy' to individuals. This isn't the case – previous legislation required consultation when making 100 staff or more redundant to begin 90 days before giving individual notice).

That's not to say that you can't start individual consultation while collective consultation is going on – in fact, if you have an urgent need to reduce costs in your organisation it would be sensible to have the two processes running at the same time – but you cannot give notice to anyone until the consultation period is up.

As mentioned earlier, you have an obligation to notify the government department responsible for employment matters if you are making more than 20 people redundant. You must do so using the same timescales as above, using form HR1, which can be downloaded from the government website (www.gov.uk).

Failing to consult can be extremely costly to your business. Individuals can claim what is known as a 'protective award' from an Employment Tribunal if you don't follow the timescale. For example, if you were planning to make 25 staff redundant, and failed to consult for the 30-day period, all 25 could claim 30 days' pay from you through the tribunal. It's no defence in this situation to argue urgency – even if it's an issue of putting the organisation into administration, staff are still entitled to consultation.

## Redundancy payments

Redundancy is one of the only situations where the law states that compensation must be paid to employees who are losing their jobs. This payment is in addition to any notice period that the employee is entitled to. Employees need at least two years' service to qualify for a redundancy payment and the payment is calculated according to a formula based on age and length of service with the organisation. (It is a minimum of two weeks' and a maximum of 30 weeks' pay). There is a table (easily available on the internet, from the Gov.uk website among others) which gives you the information as to how many weeks' pay are due, to save you having to calculate payments individually on every occasion.

This statutory redundancy also includes a 'cap' on a week's gross pay – the April 2017 rate (the current rate at the time of writing) is £489 p/w but normally changes every April. So an individual earning £500 per week and due five weeks' pay is only entitled to a redundancy payment of £2,445 (5 x £489), while an individual who earns £350 p/w and is due five weeks' pay is entitled to a redundancy payment of £1,750 (5 x £350).

Of course, you can offer more than the statutory minimum, and many organisations do. It all depends on what you can afford. What you cannot do is pay less than the statutory formula. One word of caution however – if you do want to offer a better payment scheme than the minimum you need to ensure that it isn't automatically offered on every occasion, otherwise it may become a contractual entitlement.

Redundancy payments are tax-free (provided they don't exceed £30,000) and should be paid on the last day of employment.

## Voluntary redundancy

There is no legal obligation to offer voluntary redundancy to staff before you embark on a compulsory process.

You may want to consider this as part of the process, but you need to consider the advantages and disadvantages before you do.

On the positive side, allowing volunteers to go means that compulsory redundancies are reduced or eliminated, meaning that staff who remain have not had to go through the trauma of a redundancy exercise and thus may remain better motivated. It can also mean that staff who are not happy with your organisation leave on an amicable basis and you lose some of your least committed and productive staff.

However, you need to consider the potential extra cost – since to attract volunteers you will almost certainly need to offer better terms than statutory. You will also need to think about what you will do if a key member of staff asks to leave, or if you get more volunteers than you need. And if you do refuse a request to leave, how are you going to motivate a member of staff who clearly doesn't want to be a part of your organisation?

Voluntary redundancies therefore aren't an easy option, but you may well want to consider them as part of your planning process.

## Final things to think about

To reiterate, redundancy is a form of dismissal. So, as with the other types of dismissal, you need to allow individuals a right of appeal. For these reasons, it's always useful to keep a senior manager/director or board member separate from the process in order to hear any appeals that may arise. This doesn't mean that this individual can't be part of the business decision to implement redundancies, but he or she shouldn't get involved in the decisions regarding specific individuals.

If your decision is challenged at a tribunal, the first question a tribunal will ask is whether or not this is a genuine redundancy, using the legal definition at the start of the chapter. Redundancy therefore isn't an 'easy' alternative to dealing with an underperforming staff member, or where someone has a different approach or opinion to the way the organisation wants to do things.

CHAPTER 15:

# See you in court...

Just as in life as a whole, not every working relationship ends amicably. Where matters are disputed and cannot be resolved between the employer and employee, there is legal recourse through the Employment Tribunal system – the work equivalent of the Divorce Court.

Employment Tribunals have a very negative image among employers. This is in part because the media tend to focus on the more sensational cases – usually involving some form of discrimination or where the ex-employee is claiming for hundreds of thousands of pounds. There is also a perception that the tribunal system is biased towards employees.

However, the reality is slightly different. Since 2012, employees have had to pay a high fee to enter a claim (around £1,300 if it goes to a full hearing). As a consequence, the number of tribunal claims has fallen around 70%. In fact, one recent report claimed that as a result of the fees, a small employer was likely to face a tribunal claim once every 40 years! However, the issue of tribunal fees has been legally challenged, and – at the time of writing – a Supreme Court decision is expected, so ensure you have up to date information. on this subject.

Before a tribunal will consider a claim, it has to go through an Early Conciliation process. This is where ACAS will contact both you and the individual to see if there is some way in which the claim can be settled. We will look at the process, and whether you should consider this option, later in the chapter.

Moreover, even if the claim does go all the way to a hearing, the latest figures suggest that only around half of unfair dismissal claims succeed at tribunal and the average award of compensation in such cases is around £7,000 (in fact, almost a third of successful claims don't result in any compensation). Even in discrimination cases, where compensation levels are potentially much higher, the amounts vary but typically average between £7,500 and £13,500. And while that's still a lot of money for a small organisation, it is not the lottery-style figures quoted in tabloid newspapers.

That's not to say tribunals aren't an issue for small organisations. Even if you successfully defend a claim, the time taken can be a major burden – it's not uncommon for an unfair dismissal claim to be heard six to nine months after the actual dismissal took place, and there is potentially a lot of paperwork that needs to be produced or completed, as well as the need to involve witnesses.

In addition, although the idea behind Employment Tribunals was that they would provide a quick and speedy resolution to disputes without the need for legal representation, in practice many organisations want the security of a representative, whether this comes from a lawyer, HR specialist or trade association. The costs of this representation – which can be significant – also need to be taken into account.

So, what type of thing can an individual claim through the tribunal? We've already mentioned unfair dismissal and the various forms of discrimination, but tribunals can also deal with a wide variety of claims, including those relating to breach of contract (primarily failure to pay notice correctly), equal pay, failure to carry out redundancy procedures correctly or to pay redundancy pay, unauthorised deductions from wages, claims relating to the minimum wage, and failure to comply with the Working Time Directive. For the purposes of the rest of the chapter we'll assume that you're dealing with unfair dismissal – the process is essentially the same for all claims however.

If an employee or ex-employee wishes to make a claim, he or she must – in most cases – notify ACAS at the same time, on their Early Conciliation form. Following receipt of this, ACAS will contact both you and the individual to see if there is some way in which the claim can be settled. In a lot of cases, even if you are convinced you have done everything correctly, it may be commercially sensible to settle at this point – but you are under no obligation to, and may decide that you want to contest the claim. It will depend on the circumstances of each individual case. This Early Conciliation period lasts for up to a month (it can be extended for a further two weeks if both sides agree). If the issue is resolved, a legally binding settlement is drawn up by ACAS; if not then ACAS issue a certificate to say that conciliation has not resolved the issue and the formal tribunal process can start.

This isn't to say that this is your only opportunity to reach an out of court settlement – ACAS are available at any point should you or the individual wish to discuss a possible way of resolving the issue.

Tribunal claims must normally be presented within three months of the alleged incident – so in the case of an unfair dismissal claim, a claim must be made to the tribunal within three months of the date of dismissal. Two important things to remember are that if you dismiss someone on, say, 30 June and put them on garden leave for their notice period of a month, the date of dismissal is the end of July and so they have till the end of October to make a claim. Secondly, the clock 'stops' while you are undergoing early conciliation. The tribunal system is usually very strict on deadlines, and while there are certain circumstances where it will allow an extension of time these are relatively rare.

The tribunal will analyse each claim it receives. As well as checking whether it is in time, one of the things they will look at is whether the individual has enough service with you to make a claim. An employee can make various claims – such as discrimination or breach of contract – regardless of how much or how little service they have (indeed someone who has never worked for you can enter a discrimination claim if they believe they have missed out during a recruitment exercise because they possess a 'protected characteristic' – race, sex, disability etc). Claims for unfair dismissal, redundancy etc. however currently require two years' service

Once received and accepted by the tribunal, a copy of the employee's claim will be sent to you together with the forms to enter your response. The most important thing on receiving this is not to panic! You have 28 days to enter your response and you should take time to consider how you intend to do it and to take advice. Don't leave it to the last minute to submit however as the tribunal is as strict on the response deadlines as it is on claims (again, there are limited circumstances where you may ask the tribunal to extend the deadline, but don't assume it).

The main part of your response covers your view of what happened – here is where you should refute the allegations or put forward your own explanation if the basic events are not disputed. You do not need to put in every detail at this stage, just enough to outline the grounds for disputing or rejecting the claim. On the form you will also be able to nominate a representative to deal with the matter for you if you wish.

Once you have entered this response, and it has been accepted, a tribunal judge will review both the claim and your response. Depending on what they read, they will either issue instructions to both sides about when supporting paperwork and witness statements need to be exchanged, and set a date for the hearing, or will call a pre-hearing to clarify the issues – especially if there seems to be a wide divergence of views on what has happened or if there appears a complex legal matter. As part of the same process they will ask the individual claimant to prepare a 'schedule of loss' – this is very useful as it gives you a realistic idea of what compensation might be awarded if you were to lose the claim.

Once you have the tribunal's instructions, you need to prepare all the paperwork and decide who needs to appear as a witness. Witnesses are normally the manager who dismissed the employee and the manager who heard any appeal – it's not often the case that other staff who were involved in an investigation, or the incidents leading to dismissal, need to be involved. This is because the tribunal has three things to consider: firstly, whether there is a fair reason for dismissal; secondly whether you followed a fair process (both of which we outlined in the chapters on dismissal and redundancy); and finally ,whether your decision to dismiss was reasonable given the facts of the case. This last point is very important – it is not the tribunal's job to say whether they would have dismissed in the circumstances, but whether you were justified in deciding to dismiss.

Here's an example. Mike works for a company and at Christmas brings in his own set of Christmas lights from home which he plugs in on his desk to decorate his office. They are an old set and short-circuit the offices, causing the company to have to call out an electrician to fix them. Not only has the company been hit with the repair costs, but they have also potentially lost working time. Company A takes a view that Mike didn't mean any harm and was just not thinking, and issues him with a final warning; Company B however considers that the potential fire hazard he caused and the actual problems the incident created justifies dismissing him.

At the tribunal, the panel members may think that Company B was too harsh and that, had it been down to them personally they would have taken the same view as Company A. However, their job is to decide whether Company B's decision was reasonable in the circumstances – which it could quite easily be.

Having prepared and indexed the paperwork (a job which usually falls to you as the employer, on the assumption that you have more resources) and prepared your witness statements, the next stage will normally be the hearing. (It's worth reiterating here that all through this preparation stage, in fact right up to the morning of the hearing, ACAS will be prepared to try to conciliate a settlement if you wish).

Tribunals themselves are heard at various regional centres around the country and the case will normally be heard at the centre nearest to the place the employee worked before dismissal. Only in the most complicated of cases – or where there are multiple claimants and thus potentially a lot of witnesses – will a hearing normally be scheduled for more than a day.

The hearing is chaired by an employment judge, a fully qualified employment lawyer who may work full or part-time for the tribunal. In most cases, they will be the only person hearing the claim but occasionally, he or she may be assisted by two lay members (sometimes referred to as 'wing members') one of whom is a representative of employers (often nominated by organisations such as the CBI or FSB, for instance) and the other a representative of employees (frequently retired trade union officers).

The tribunal is a court and needs to be treated with the same degree of respect and formality as any other law court. Witnesses give their statements on oath (and could be prosecuted for perjury if found to be lying). However, there are no wigs and gowns and the proceedings can be conducted in a more relaxed fashion – employment judges are normally very willing to explain the procedures and put witnesses at ease, particularly if either side is not represented. Overly-aggressive cross-examination is also generally frowned on. In the hearing, the ex-employee bringing the case is known as the 'claimant' while you are known as the 'respondent'.

Having heard all the witnesses and allowing both you and the individual to present a summary of your case, the judge will withdraw to consider their decision. Unless the case has run very late in the day, or if there is some controversy or legal issue which takes a lot of time to resolve, both sides will be called back in and given the decision on the same day. If the decision cannot be delivered the same day, it is known as a 'reserved' decision and will be sent to you later in writing.

If you win – i.e. the tribunal dismisses the claim – that is the end of the matter.

If you lose, the tribunal will award compensation to the individual. The way in which this is done is explained below, but they will either award compensation on the day or schedule a 'remedy hearing' – which typically takes around an hour – some weeks later. In this latter case, you may want to try to negotiate a settlement via ACAS in the intervening period.

Also if you lose, the judge will outline why the tribunal has reached its decision in detail (you can ask for this to be provided in writing too). It is always worth taking note of this as it will explain to you what 'went wrong' and what you can do to prevent it happening again.

If the tribunal do award compensation this is done in three parts:

- A Basic Award – calculated in exactly the same way as a redundancy payment (see Chapter 14), including the limit of £489 (April 2017) per week.

- A Compensatory Award - this is based on how much the employee has lost through being dismissed (which is based on their net not gross pay). Any income the employee gains since losing their job will be deducted (including any unemployment benefit that has been paid) so if the employee has got a new job on a similar salary compensation can be limited; if on the other hand they are still unemployed or have had to take a low paid job the tribunal can award an estimated loss of future earnings as well. They can also take into account loss of things such as pension rights. If you have blatantly ignored the basic ACAS advice on disciplinary procedures (outlined in Chapter 13) they can increase the compensation by up to 25%. However, they can reduce any compensation if the employee 'contributed to his own downfall' – for example if you dismissed an employee for theft but got the process wrong, the tribunal can take the view that he would have been dismissed anyway if you had done it fairly and reduce any compensation accordingly. They can also reduce compensation by up to 25% if the employee fails to use your internal procedures (e.g. fails to appeal).

- An Additional Award – in some cases, although increasingly rare, the employee may want their old job back and the tribunal may issue a reinstatement order. If you fail to reinstate someone after being ordered to do so (which would be entirely understandable as it's very difficult to build up a working relationship with someone in this situation) then extra compensation of between 26 and 52 weeks' pay – again capped at £489 per week – can be awarded.

- Any fees that the individual has had to pay to enter the claim (which could be around £1,300). However, you won't – except in the most unusual of circumstances – be liable for any legal fees they have incurred. (Equally you won't be able to reclaim any legal fees you have incurred, even if you win).

If they lose a tribunal, many employers naturally feel very aggrieved and want to know if they can appeal against the decision. The answer to this is in theory yes – but, in practice, no.

You can only appeal to the Employment Appeals Tribunal (usually just known as the EAT) if the tribunal has:

a) Made a legal mistake (e.g. misinterpreted a piece of legislation or case law);

b) Substituted their own view of what should have happened rather than considered whether your decision was reasonable;

c) Reached a conclusion that is 'perverse', i.e. that no-one, based on the evidence heard, could reasonably have reached.

Just disagreeing with the conclusion of the tribunal is not sufficient reason. Even if you do think that you have a case, the time and particularly the costs of going to the EAT can be prohibitive for all but the largest organisations. You also need to remember that one option open to the EAT, if they rule in your favour, is to send the case back to be reheard by a different tribunal panel – which means that you have to go through the full hearing again and still might lose!

Tribunals are, on the whole, an unpleasant and nerve-wracking experience for everyone involved (including the ex-employee who brings the case as well as you) so you may be wondering if there is any way to avoid them. There are two ways in which you can do this.

The first involves ACAS, and is very similar to the role they play in a tribunal claim. If you have an employee you have dismissed and you want to pre-empt a claim, or if you are thinking of dismissing and would prefer to the individual to leave 'quietly', you can contact ACAS who will then – for free – undertake a similar conciliation role, with the aim of trying to reach a settlement between you and your employee. If such an agreement is reached, one of the conditions is that it is in 'full and final settlement' of any potential tribunal claims – in other words the employee is signing away their legal rights to make a tribunal claim in return for some form of compensation.

One thing that ACAS will not do however is to 'rubber stamp' a deal you have already agreed with your employee – there must be an actual or potential dispute and disagreement which they can resolve.

The other option is to negotiate what is called a 'Settlement Agreement'. The general principle is the same – you give the employee some money and they sign away their right to make a tribunal claim - but there are two key differences. The first is that the employee must be advised by an appropriate solicitor who must also countersign the agreement (there are a very limited number of other advisers who can take this role); the second is that it is common – though not compulsory - for the employer to make a contribution towards the employee's costs. Although it's not necessary for you as the employer to be legally represented, it's not uncommon so there may also be costs on your side.

Depending on the nature of the issue, and the solicitor concerned, it may be possible to agree the terms with the employee and then have a solicitor countersign it.

One important word of warning: if the potential issue involves any suggestion of discrimination, be careful before you use a Settlement Agreement. This is because the Equality Act was very poorly worded and suggests that a solicitor who advises an individual cannot be independent and sign such an agreement (without which it is not binding). Even the Law Society has issued very cautious advice to solicitors. To protect yourself as an employer, always go with ACAS in such a situation.

The Employment Tribunal system is, unfortunately, a necessary evil for employers. While you may have done everything properly and, rightly, feel upset and angry that your decision has been challenged and you have to defend it, not every employer is as scrupulous as you are. There are still some who believe that employees have no rights, that they can ride roughshod over the law and treat people like cattle. While such employers still exist, there will still be a need for a legal recourse for employees. The system however is not weighted in employees' favour – nor is it a blank cheque even when an employee wins.

PART 4

# The Extended Family

CHAPTER 16:

# TUPE

Apart from 'constructive dismissal', no phrase strikes more fear into owners of small businesses, nor is more misunderstood, than 'TUPE'.

Firstly, a note on pronunciation. TUPE is generally pronounced 'chew-pee' – not 'choop' or 'toupee' – and is one of those acronyms that has become a word in itself, sometimes as a verb: 'He was tuped across in 2006' and sometimes as an adjective: 'We're in a tupe situation'.

TUPE stands for the *Transfer of Undertakings (Protection of Employment) Regulations,* which apply where a business or organisation (or a distinct part of one - for example a department or a contract) is transferred from one owner to another. For TUPE to apply, the activities before and after the transfer must be 'fundamentally the same'.

Like much of employment law, the basic premise is very simple. If you work for Company X, and it is taken over by Company Y – something over which you have no control as an employee – you should not lose your employment rights or terms and conditions just because of the takeover. TUPE applies to a transfer caused by a sale of a company (including the death of the owner), and whether the owner is an individual, a partnership or a limited company. It also applies if Company X loses a contract in a tender situation to Company Y. It does not apply where the transfer is made by share transfer (since in this case Company X still exists, it is just that its shares are owned by Company Y rather than the original owner), or when just assets are transferred. 'Undertaking' does not simply mean an organisation run for profit – voluntary organisations and charities are also covered by the regulations. TUPE only applies to employees, not to other types of worker.

The regulations themselves have been around for over 30 years and the 2014 version – the most recent amendment at the time of writing – clarified a number of uncertainties in previous regulations.

Examples of the sorts of situations where TUPE might apply include a company deciding to outsource its customer services to a third party; a local authority ending its grounds maintenance contract with one company and awarding it to another; or a bank switching its mortgage conveyancing service from one firm of solicitors to another. TUPE can apply even if there is only one employee provided there is a clear 'undertaking' that is transferring (for example an office cleaner in one building).

In the event of a TUPE transfer, a new employer is required to employ all staff employed in the business and to observe all contractual terms and conditions of employment, as well as any statutory protection which applied to employees of the transferred company before the transfer, other than terms relating to occupational pension schemes. There are, however, separate rules on pensions, which are described later. Employees also have the right not to suffer 'material detriment' as a result of a transfer, which is discussed at the end of the chapter.

If a fundamental change to the contract is made as a result of the transfer, the employee may leave and claim constructive dismissal. It would then be down to an employment tribunal to decide whether the dismissal was unfair.

An employee who is dismissed either before or after such a transfer will *automatically* be treated as having been unfairly dismissed if the transfer (or a reason connected with it) was the cause of dismissal. Automatically unfair, as we saw before, means there is no way that an employer can justify it.

Except that in a TUPE situation there can be! If the employer can show there is an economic, technical or organisational (ETO) reason requiring changes in the workforce and this – rather than the transfer itself - is the main reason for dismissal, they can defend a claim. We'll give you some examples below. In this case, the fairness of the dismissal would be tested under the normal unfair dismissal rules and the employee would need to satisfy normal qualifying conditions.

Examples of an 'economic reason' might include a shortfall in funding or a drop in demand, meaning that there needs to be a reduction in the number of employees. 'Technical reasons' cover the introduction of new machinery or methods of working which result in the existing employees not having the necessary skills or expertise, while 'organisational reasons' covers situations where the merging of transferring staff into existing structures results in a surplus or overlapping of responsibilities – for example, you might find yourself with two finance clerks doing the same job. Simply wanting to harmonise different sets of terms and conditions between staff you transfer in and your existing staff does not (in itself) constitute a valid organisational reason.

If you are the old employer (i.e. the one who is losing staff), then you have a legal responsibility to provide the new employer with details of all staff, their contractual entitlements and any other employment liabilities – like disciplinary records, time taken off on maternity leave – no later than 28 days before the transfer is due to take place. You must also carry out individual consultation with affected employees before the transfer, explaining what is happening to them. If you employ more than ten staff, there is also a requirement to consult with 'appropriate representatives' – who might be union representatives but can also be employees elected by their colleagues. Individual consultation on its own is fine if you have ten staff or fewer.

In this collective consultation, you are required to give specific information to the representatives, including information on when and why the transfer is taking place, any legal or social implications arising from it (for example, staff will be based at the new employer's depot, rather than yours), and any plans the new employer has for changes which will affect the employees who are transferring. It is essential that this consultation is done as there are potentially large tribunal awards that can be made if it is not – even if the fault is solely that of the old employer some or all of the liability, depending on the circumstances, may transfer to the new employer.

If you are the new employer (i.e. the one gaining new staff) you must provide details of any changes you are intending to make after the transfer to the old employer, before the transfer takes place, so that the old employer can include this in their consultation. This might include things like change of work location, amendments to non-contractual arrangements etc, as well as more significant issues such as redundancies justified for an ETO reason. There is no requirement for you to meet your new staff or consult with them before the transfer.

In practice however, what often happens is that both old and new employer carry out consultation sessions before the transfer takes place. Sometimes the new employer is invited to attend the collective consultation as well as individual ones. This is a very sensible idea – it can reassure employees who are transferring and also allows the new employer to meet their new employees and identify any issues they may face after the transfer.

As the new employer, you are required to take all staff employed in the undertaking transferring to you. You cannot pick and choose. It sometimes happens that you may inherit someone who has previously worked for you, who you have dismissed or would be unhappy to re-employ. Under TUPE however you have to take them.

There are two exceptions to this situation: casual staff – i.e. those who work 'as and when' required and do not have a contract of employment – have no rights under TUPE, while as we noted above, self-employed/freelance/contractors are also not protected (although you may wish to retain individuals who fall into in either category, depending on the type of contract). Similarly in an insolvency situation (for example if you buy a company or a section of a company from the receiver), certain liabilities may not pass to the new employer and it may be easier to change the terms and conditions of staff that transfer – depending on the formal legal nature of the insolvency arrangement.

As mentioned above, there is no requirement to replicate the outgoing employer's pension scheme or to allow individuals to retain membership of it. Under the Pensions Act (not the TUPE regulations) the new employer has to provide a pension meeting defined minimum standards if the previous employer provided a pension. For example, if you were taking on employees who have a final salary scheme you do not have to offer an identical scheme. However, you would have to contribute 6% of salary to a pension scheme for the transferred workers. With pension auto-enrolment coming into force, you would have to automatically enter anyone transferring to your own scheme, but you will need to be aware of the scheme that they had with their previous employer.

So far, so good. The basic principle of TUPE is very clear, and the process, although it can be time-consuming, is relatively straightforward. But where TUPE becomes complicated is in the detail. We've already seen above that the definition of an 'undertaking' can include a single person. But what about where there is a dispute over who is to transfer? Or if a company cannot replicate terms and conditions exactly? Or if you have already identified that you need to make redundancies in advance of the transfer? And what do you do if a member of staff refuses to transfer?

The regulations refer to employees who are 'wholly or mainly' employed on the work to be transferred. Wholly is pretty easy to define, being someone who works on a particular account or work area all the time. So if you run a contract cleaning company and have five cleaners working on an office block, then if you lose the contract to another company all five cleaners will transfer to them. But if you had also have a supervisor who spends some of her time supervising that office block and some of her time supervising other cleaners elsewhere, she might have the right to be transferred. How do you – either as the old or new employer – make that decision?

There are a number of tests that tribunals have defined which you need to look at. Firstly – and most simply – how much time does the individual spend on the work that is transferring? And just as importantly, is the employee part of an 'organised group' whose purpose is to carry the transferring work?

The second test is how much value does the employee give to different parts of the business? If the contract that is transferring represents 70% by income of the employee's workload, then they may have the right to transfer (even if it doesn't take up 70% of their time).

Next, you need to look at what the employee's contract requires them to do. So, if the contract required them to supervise one office block but the individual was temporarily moved to another (for example to cover a period of sickness) and the first block is transferred, the individual might have a right to transfer with it.

The final question is how the costs are allocated. Again using this example, if a majority of the supervisor's costs are allocated to the office block that is transferring – regardless of whether she spends the majority of her time on it – then she may have the right to transfer.

This question of 'assignment', as it's known in legal circles, is one of the most complicated aspects of TUPE, and it has taken many years and a considerable number of court cases to clarify the issue. It's not impossible for old and new employer to disagree over whether someone should be assigned, or for an employee to argue that they should be transferred when the old employer does not (or vice versa). Ultimately, if the dispute cannot be resolved, it may end up in an employment tribunal to be decided, but you should work through the tests above to decide on the strength of your argument. Obviously, if you are the new employer you are in a much weaker position as you will probably not have access to much of the information, but that does not mean that you cannot argue the case successfully. This is one area where if a dispute arises you should get professional advice at the earliest opportunity.

If you are the old employer, and the view is that the employee is not assigned to be transferred, then you have to take a view about whether they are potentially redundant, and if so follow the procedures in the redundancy chapter (Chapter 14).

There may be certain situations where, as the new employer, you cannot provide the same benefits as the old employer. Again, following a court case, there is now clearer guidance. The test case involved Sainsbury's supermarkets, which offered a share option scheme to staff based on the company profits. As part of an outsourcing exercise, a group of staff were transferred out to a new employer. The staff raised the question of their lost share options and argued that they were suffering reduced terms and conditions as a result. The new employer – who did operate a bonus scheme – pointed out that it was impossible for them to offer shares options in a completely separate company, and they also could not be bound to pay a bonus based on the profits of a company over which they had no control.

The courts agreed with the employer, saying that TUPE did not mean that an absurd or unjust conclusion should be reached. They did however state that the new employer had to provide a benefit that was 'substantially equivalent' to the benefit that was being lost. This might therefore mean that a new employer has to set up a bonus scheme just for employees transferred to it under TUPE, or run a separate scheme for such staff.

If you are the new employer, you may have already identified that you will have too many staff before the transfer takes effect. In the past, you legally had to transfer all the relevant staff from the old employer and then, if necessary, start a redundancy process (see Chapter 13). However, quite apart from the business consequences, the upset of transferring staff from one business to another – which can be difficult for people involved in the transfer, especially if they had worked for the old employer for some time – and then telling them they were at risk of losing their job, is not a great way to start a new employment relationship.

So, since 2014, if you are aware that you need to undergo a redundancy process (and have an ETO reason – see above – to justify it), and have informed the old employer of this, you can start the consultation process before the transfer. In certain situations this might mean that individuals leave on redundancy terms without ever formally transferring to you; if it is as a result of your decision you are still liable for the costs.

You may encounter a situation where an employee who is due to transfer objects to being transferred. Employees have a perfect right to do this (as no-one can be forced to work for a company they do not wish to). However, in such a situation, the contract between the old employer and the individual simply ends on the date of transfer – there is no dismissal (and hence no risk of an unfair dismissal claim) nor is there any liability for a redundancy payment. If this situation does arise, as the old employer you would be well advised to ensure that the individual understands the consequences of what they are doing (including directing them to get advice if necessary), confirms their objection to you in writing and also ensure that you advise the new employer of the situation.

One of the issues mentioned above is that employees are entitled not to receive a 'material detriment' as a result of a transfer. In a nutshell, this means that where an employee is made substantially worse off, even though the employer has not breached the contract, the employee may have grounds to resign and claim constructive dismissal.

In the past, one of the most common material detriments was a requirement for employees to change their workplace (e.g. from the old employer's offices to yours). Again, since 2014, this is no longer an automatically unfair dismissal. Provided you can justify the need to change the workplace with an ETO reason (which ought to be relatively straightforward in many cases) you can expect staff to move, even if this causes them some inconvenience.

Although TUPE can become complicated, it's important to remember that most TUPE situations are clear and straightforward. Provided there is a reasonable degree of co-operation between the old employer and the new one, most transfers go ahead with minimal difficulty. While there are some legal pitfalls to avoid, most problems actually arise where the old employer and the new one do not work together (for example where Company A has lost a vital contract to its biggest rival, Company B).

CHAPTER 17:

# Trade unions

For many people – especially those over 40 – the phrase 'trade union' conveys images of Arthur Scargill-like demagogues; shop stewards ready to take workers out on strike if a manager looked at them in the wrong way, or violence on picket lines. The reality today – despite a number of recent high-profile disputes - is completely different, but that brings with it additional and different issues for many small organisations.

The 1970s image of unions has led many people to think they're a bad thing in the workplace, so it's worth remembering that in the 19th century, the control of the employment relationship was solely in the hands of the employer – this was the era when children worked in factories, employees could be fired and blacklisted (barred from working at other employers in the same area) at will and were subject to long hours and poor working conditions. Even Adam Smith, the economist often quoted in support of free markets and deregulation, noted that there was an imbalance of rights in favour of employers and against employees.

Trade unions were established to counter this imbalance, by promoting the collective power of the workforce. Given that workers had little in the way of negotiating power, their only weapon was to withdraw their labour – or strike. Gradually over the course of the 20th century unionisation increased and working conditions improved. In some cases, unions were able to negotiate a 'closed shop', where an individual had to be a union member to secure employment. Over the same period, unions also began to offer their members many other benefits, such as savings schemes, education and training.

The increased role and influence of unions, coupled with the activities of some politically motivated union leaders, led many to consider that the balance of power had swung too much in the workers' direction, and a series of trade union reforms in the 1980s – including outlawing the 'closed shop' – resulted in a significant reduction in both union membership and influence. But it's important to remember that unions still do have certain legal rights and privileges – as well as responsibilities – and individuals who are union members also have certain legal protections.

The most fundamental right is that an employee has the right to belong to a trade union or not, and not to suffer any form of detriment from their employer as a result of that decision. To discriminate against an employee solely on the grounds that they are or are not a union member is automatically unfair and is one of those areas where an employee requires no service to bring a claim against you. Similarly, employees who wish to organise a local branch of the union, encourage others to join or who hold a position in the union are also protected. Employees do not have the right to coerce colleagues into union membership, nor do they have any right to take time off during working hours to carry out union activities if your organisation does not recognise a union. 'Recognition' of a trade union is a particular legal term, which we'll cover later.

As already mentioned in earlier chapters, employees also have the right in certain circumstances – formal grievance or disciplinary hearings, for example – to be accompanied by a trade union representative, regardless of whether your organisation is unionised. And in certain collective issues – for example redundancy and TUPE – staff may want to have union representation.

Many small organisations do not have trade union representation. However, as noted above, this does not mean that you will never encounter union representatives. Some industries and sectors are more highly unionised and so dealing with unions becomes more commonplace. However, the 'problem' for many managers in small organisations is that, as union membership has declined, they rarely if ever deal with a union official and are unsure of how to do so when on the infrequent occasions it does happen. Coupled with the perception of unions that lingers from the 1970s, this results in 'the trade union' becoming something of a bogeyman to them.

The first thing to make clear is that modern unions do not, on the whole, operate like those in the 1970s. That said, they will approach any meeting with you from a different perspective. Yours is to carry out something that you see as necessary for your business – theirs is to represent and defend their member(s) interests. Different representatives will carry this out in different ways, although it has to be said that the table-thumping intransigent shop steward of the past is very much a dying breed. Most union representatives these days will approach a meeting with you in a professional way and look to maintain a constructive relationship. They have no desire to protect 'bad apples' that you want to dismiss, and usually recognise the realities of the situation if you are faced with redundancies.

What they will do however is ensure that you follow procedures correctly, and will seek to get the best for their members in difficult situations. So, in a redundancy situation, the union may accept that you need to make redundancies but argue for enhanced redundancy terms or wider redeployment opportunities, etc. They're not normally looking to pick a fight with you, but create a solution that benefits their members.

Think of dealing with unions in this context as though you were negotiating a new sales deal. There is always a bit of give and take in such circumstances, and you rarely come away with everything you want – but a successful sales negotiation gives both parties the feeling that they have gained something. It's exactly the same if you have to discuss issues with a union.

So who exactly are the unions these days? Like many organisations faced with decline, there have been a raft of mergers in recent years and, rather than represent a single or group of trades, the biggest in the UK now are general unions more akin to their counterparts in Europe. Many well-known union names have disappeared and so you are unlikely to encounter the 'Amalgamated Union of Fettlers, Warp and Web Adjusters' and more likely to meet a representative from one of the 'Big Three':

UNISON – primarily represents workers in local government and the health service, but has considerable numbers of members who work in the voluntary sector. If you bid for public sector work you may well encounter them.

UNITE – formed from the merger of the Transport and General Workers with engineering and 'white collar' unions, this has members across both private and public sectors.

GMB – again predominantly public sector, particularly among manual workers, but with competitive tendering and other contracting out of public sector work it has a strong base in certain parts of the private sector.

Together these three represent around 3.5 million workers, or nearly 55% of those who are union members in the UK.

We referred earlier to the concept of trade union recognition. This refers to a situation where you, as the employer, negotiate wages and terms and conditions of employment with a union rather than with staff direct. It can either be done on a voluntary basis, where you agree that a union (or unions) can negotiate on behalf of staff, or on a statutory basis. Statutory recognition is extremely rare with small organisations (it only applies if you have 21 or more employees), but involves a legal process. Essentially, if a union can show that either in the workforce as a whole, or within a particular 'bargaining unit' (eg a particular factory or a group of workers) it represents a majority of workers, then it's legally entitled to representation. There are a variety of legal tests it must follow but if it can pass them then you as the employer have no choice but to recognise it.

If a union is recognised, there are additional responsibilities that fall on you as the employer. These include the right to time off with pay for local representatives (often but not always known as shop stewards) to carry out their union duties (such as being involved in negotiations) and to undertake training by the union to carry these out. They are also allowed a certain amount of unpaid time off for what are called union activities, such as organising union meetings, or meeting with full time trade union officers.

What many employers fear is that union involvement will lead to the use of the ultimate weapon – the strike. In fact, industrial action of any kind (including overtime bans, so-called 'work to rule', as well as strikes) is fairly rare, especially in smaller organisations. It can only occur if every attempt to reach agreement fails, and after the union holds a properly constituted ballot in which a majority approve strike action. It is not usually something that a union wants to do any more than you as an employer want it to happen.

In conclusion, unions are something that you may never encounter, but if you do they're nothing to be overly concerned about, and in fact – as with your employees – if you develop a positive working relationship with them, their involvement can be an asset to your business, not a hindrance.

# CHAPTER 18:

# Happily ever after

Having reached the end of the book, you might be thinking that managing people effectively seems quite complex. In some respects, it is. People are creative, inspirational, exciting and dynamic. They are also irritating, obstinate, uncooperative and rude. And you are a person too, so, at times, you will also be all of these things.

As a result, to be a successful people manager requires you to recognise your own personality traits and those of the people you work with, and adapt to them. Although this is sometimes derided as a 'soft skill', I'd suggest this is far harder to do effectively than, say, manage finances or property.

It's worth remembering five key points:

- You must have trust and confidence in your employees – but they must also have trust and confidence in you;

- For many small organisations, the people you employ are your biggest cash investment. You need to make sure you get the best return from them, and that means managing them effectively;

- A small minority of employees are troublesome and litigious. The overwhelming majority want to do a decent job for a decent salary, and in many cases will want to develop their own career. Don't let the tiny minority have a significant influence on the way you manage the majority;

- Despite what you may have read, employment law doesn't prevent you doing many things (like sacking under-performing staff, or making essential changes to the way your business runs). What it does do, however, is insist that you do not behave in an arbitrary manner and that you have a supportable business reason for your decisions;

- You are very unlikely (or unlucky!) to encounter all of the different situations described in this book at the same time. In fact, some small organisations may never have to deal with some of them – for example, having to deal with an Employment Tribunal claim.

Managing the people who work for you is as important for your organisation as controlling your costs, having a marketing plan or developing quality systems. It's a skill that all business leaders need (wherever they work) and – whatever the legal framework – doing it effectively will make sure that you create a successful and sustainable organisation.

# Further information

A book like this can only skim the surface of the variety of people management and employment law topics. There's a lot of freely available information on the internet these days (make sure you always check it is from a reliable source, like the sites listed below), which will give you more detail – although you need to remember that if you have a specific problem it's always helpful to get advice.

Some useful sites are:

- **www.acas.org.uk** ACAS can provide you with a wealth of resources and their helpline is available to both employers and employees.

- **www.gov.uk/employing-people** is the Government's site that gives you plenty of good information on employment issues. It is (understandably) fairly general in what it covers and is aimed at explaining things for both employers and employees. Other sections of the gov.uk site are also helpful – for example you can also find information here on the current rules about work visas, should you be looking to recruit non-UK staff.

- **https://knowhownonprofit.org/people/employment-law-and-hr** is a helpful site, developed by the National Council for Voluntary Organisations (NCVO). It's aimed at charities and other 'not-for-profit' organisations, and you may need to be an NCVO member in order to access certain parts of the site.

- **www.belbin.com** will give you more information on Belbin team types, including information on how to access their tools to identify your own type(s).

If you are interested in reading more about the management and motivation theories referred to in the book, then the following are recommended:

Charles B. Handy – **Understanding Organisations** (4th Edition, Penguin 1993). One of the classic books which gives you a clear overview of management theory

Kenneth Blanchard and Spencer Johnson – **The One Minute Manager** (Harper 2000). The first of a whole series of books around situational leadership, it's a very quick and easy read

Daniel Pink – **Drive: The Surprising Truth About What Motivates Us** (Canongate Books, 2011) An interesting and easy to read book about money, motivation and the links between the two

R.Meredith Belbin – **Management Teams – why they succeed or fail** (3rd Edition, Butterworth – Heinemann 2010). Belbin's original research, it contains the full descriptions of the different team roles.

## About the Author

Simon Jones is an experienced Human Resources professional who set up and runs Ariadne Associates, an HR consultancy which provides a wide range of HR support to small and medium businesses and voluntary organisations.

In addition to over 30 years' HR and management experience, gained in both private and public sector organisations, Simon is a Fellow of the Chartered Institute of Personnel and Development (CIPD) and holds an MA in Strategic Human Resources Management from Liverpool John Moores University. As well as running his business, he is an associate tutor for CIPD programmes with MOL (www.mollearn.com), one of the UK's leading professional qualifications providers.

In addition to Happy Working Relationships, Simon has contributed to two successful anthologies of HR writings, 'Humane, Resourced' and 'This Time it's Personnel', both available as Amazon e-books.

Simon lives in Liverpool with his wife and daughter.

You can visit his website at www.ariadne-associates.co.uk and follow him on Twitter @ariadneassoc.

118

#0242 - 240417 - C0 - 210/148/7 - PB - DID1822440